It's well that a picture tells a thousand words, for Lt John Rosel would never speak of the frenzy of desert combat. He let his camera tell the story of his 2/24th Battalion's odyssey from northern Victoria to its costly blooding in the Siege of Tobruk.

Although Rosel left no diaries, and letters to his girlfriend Lorna did not survive, we're fortunate that he pencilled notes on the back of some photos – endearments, names, places, some pithy comments. While his family shared a handful of his 600-plus images with the Australian War Memorial decades ago, the approaching 80th anniversary of the Siege in 2021 inspired them to make additional photographs more widely known. John Rosel and the mates who shared his camera left a legacy of Australians in peace and war: in training, exploring exotic lands, sheltering in dugouts, digging, writing letters, eating fly-harassed meals in the open desert …

Complementing Rosel's story are never-before-published letters by Private Harry Frazer, bandsman turned rifleman in Rosel's platoon. Harry's intimate, frank letters to his parents are among the most moving human documents of the Siege.

These wartime images and recollections echo the experience of millions: love of country, of comrades, of man and woman, parents for children, and children for parents.

Lt John Rosel, Bonegilla army camp, Victoria, 1940.

A RAT OF TOBRUK

A DIGGER'S LOST IMAGES OF THE SIEGE

MIKE ROSEL

ARCADIA

First published 2020 by
Australian Scholarly Publishing Pty Ltd
7 Lt Lothian St Nth, North Melbourne, Vic 3051
Tel: 03 9329 6963 / Fax: 03 9329 5452
enquiry@scholarly.info / www.scholarly.info

ISBN 978-1-925984-74-3 PB

ISBN 978-1-925984-77-4 HB

Cover design: Wayne Saunders

Front Cover: Tobruk, May 1941. Lt John Rosel with a field telephone in a sangar, a rock defensive breastwork part of perimeter Post S10, where he won the Military Cross in the Battle of the Salient, April 30–2 May.

Back cover: A reflective Lt John Rosel in a perimeter post at Tobruk, June 1941. *I was thinking of you pet* is his note on the back of this photo sent to his girlfriend Lorna.

Dedication

To the memory of the three intrepid Rößel brothers and their sister drawn from their villages in Lower Saxony to Victorian goldfields from 1854. Immigration officials anglicised their name. Seventeen years later Bismarck unified Germany and set his nation on its militaristic march.

Again, to my patient and supportive family, especially my wife Maureen, born to be a compassionate Commanding Officer.

And a salute to my father, the calm, strong man whose photographs (and those of his mates who returned the favour) are now to reach beyond our family on the 80th anniversary of the Tobruk siege. To his comrades, especially those who contributed to the battalion history which made this book possible.

John Rosel's children would agree with the English poet Chaucer, writing of another warrior almost 600 years earlier: 'A verray parfit gentil knyghte.'

CONTENTS

PROLOGUE

'A SUNLIT PICTURE OF HELL'

Lieutenant John Rosel, pencil in one hand, inevitable cigarette in the other, was drawing up a potentially lethal ledger.

The North African sun burned down on Post S10 and its two sister posts on the perimeter defences of the Libyan coastal town of Tobruk.

No great reader, he may never have seen what another Lieutenant, the British war poet Siegfried Sassoon, had written on 1 July 1916 after witnessing the unprecedented slaughter of the first day of the Battle of the Somme: 'A sunlit picture of hell.'

But this was mid-afternoon, May 1, 1941, and his 14 Platoon of 'C' Company of the 2/24th Battalion was confronting its own looming hell.

Lacking a Field Message form, he improvised by ripping pages from his diary.

This was a central episode in the Siege of Tobruk, where Australian and British troops resisted their German and Italian enemies for eight months.

Nothing seen against a war that would cost some 75 million soldiers' and civilian lives. But my father, John Rosel, 24, was hardly thinking of grand strategies of global war, or of British Prime Minister Churchill telling Australians that 'the whole Empire is watching'. Forget how his mates had appropriated 'The Rats of Tobruk' – the propaganda slur of Germany's broadcaster 'Lord Haw-Haw' – and made it a badge of honour that would become a legend.

No time to look at the photos of his girlfriend Lorna Knowles in faraway Melbourne, or use the folding camera which had documented the odyssey of his Victorian battalion from training days at Wangaratta and Bonegilla to the Middle East.

For John, sometimes 'Jack' or 'Johnny', had a ledger to balance, the Battle of the Salient to continue, and the former National Bank clerk born in the tiny Wimmera village of Natimuk was just the Digger to do it.

It was terse copy, lots of Army abbreviations, not quite Hemingway's spare prose, more that of a tabloid reporter. Yet it was to become one of the most-reproduced documents of the siege which had immense symbolism as the first significant reverse to German arms.

Here is a synopsis of his Situation Report (see 'A Message from Our Father' for the full version).

On the credit side: some 30 members of his platoon. (Men yet to be tried in battle, but sustained by the tradition of ANZAC, they knew the mutual support called mateship, when men overcame fear, unwilling to let their friends down, or to be seen to let them down. He had a good officer's love for his platoon, Shakespeare's 'band of brothers': 60 years later, a fellow officer would put it perfectly – 'He nurtured them'.)

His sums continued:

Bren guns.

Breda light machine guns (captured Italian weapons, cursed for jamming when desert sand got into the device which oiled each cartridge as it entered the chamber).

An Italian mortar.

One Boyes .55-inch antitank rifle (a beast to fire, well nicknamed 'the elephant gun', but useless against medium tanks).

He added up thousands of .303 rounds, mortar bombs, ballistite rounds for rifle grenades. Food enough for two days (if they lived that long).

Known lifelong for his mantra 'If a job's worth doing, it's worth doing well!' he even listed the five German prisoners in Post S8, 'one being badly wounded.'

He didn't need to mention the ubiquitous .303 Lee Enfield rifles carried by every soldier.

The debits, rather daunting:

The enemy had a light gun (an artillery piece) and mortar on a ridge, making one of his posts untenable. No communications. Some 200 enemy digging in nearby. Wire worthless.

The account balance: 'The position tonight is going to be very serious and if some reinforcements could be produced we would stand a fair chance … Here's hoping.' Stiff upper lip?

But there were three startling words before that summary: 'Viva la Batallion' (*sic*).

Here, surely, was defiance in the face of disaster, emotion for his own men and the battalion. Perhaps a hint of the reputed gladiators' cry in ancient Rome: *Morituri te salutant.* 'We who are about to die salute you.' Forgive his misspelling of battalion: his blood was up. If the account balanced, they might survive; if it 'got into the red' – the customary bankers' indicator of an overdrawn balance – the red would be blood.

Lt Rosel scribbled a conclusion at 15.40 (3.40pm) and ended with his usual signature flourish.

He sent the message off with Corporal James 'Bluey' Jackson, who had earlier brought him ammunition from the neighbouring 2/23rd Battalion. John Rosel, like millions of soldiers worldwide, then waited for imminent assault, and the verdict of combat and history.

The British war poet Wilfred Owen had described troops facing oblivion: 'Knowing their feet had come to the edge of the world.' That edge was barely four hours off.

Mike Rosel, 2020

THE PHOTOGRAPHS

The 600-plus photographs of Lt John Rosel MC give a soldier's perspective, literally, of the 2/24th Battalion's service in Australia and the Middle East in WWII, with particular focus on the Siege of Tobruk.

My father went to war armed with a .303 rifle, a pistol and a folding camera. He filled two albums with small prints typically only 80 x 50 mm. While no negatives survive, we can scan details from the prints thanks to the Zeiss lens on his camera and bright desert light.

He didn't have the professionalism, equipment, access or propaganda priorities of the notable Department of Information photographers who recorded the siege in its late stages – Damien Parer, George Silk, and Frank Hurley. No heroic poses, no arty angles. John focussed on his platoon and the humble, often harsh and necessarily simple life of the Digger. Most are snaps of mates for everyone's families. His colleagues then turned the camera on him for photos for his Lorna, family and friends, leaving us a priceless legacy of dad in the desert. Decades later we made some of the key photographs available to the Australian War Memorial.

If a picture is famously worth 1,000 words, these pictures had to do the talking, for his six kids quickly discovered he would never speak of combat, even in the most intimate setting. As he told one of my friends, in our teen years: 'Don't ask about *that*.' Those of us who subsequently became interested in military history in an attempt to understand what dad, and millions, had endured, quickly discovered a common response among combat survivors: 'If you weren't there, you couldn't know.'

The first album in its black cover recorded the 2/24th Battalion training at Wangaratta and Bonegilla and tracked its passage to the Middle East via the exotic attractions of Colombo in Ceylon (Sri Lanka).

The second album, presumably bought in a Cairo bazaar, has a colourful leather cover embossed with hieroglyphics and the bust of Nefertiti. Within are places familiar to tens of thousands of Diggers of two wars: Egypt, Palestine, Syria and more. The last images are newspaper photos of John's 1942 reunion with Lorna, by now his fiancé.

Here are tired Diggers sprawled on a road outside Bonegilla, taking a 10-minute smoko during a route march as they morphed from civilian volunteers to fit Diggers; here is dad leaning on a shovel – truly a Digger – or taking a hip bath; cropping and blow-ups record bayonet training and unarmed combat. The cover photo captures him chatting on a field telephone in Post S10, where he was to lead his platoon and fight off repeated attacks. Turn the print over: *My first home up here, darling.*

Carefully lift many images from photo corners 80 years old and you find more pencilled comments, sometimes name and place captions, or an endearment for Lorna. These have to serve for insights into his Army life. If he kept a diary, it didn't survive, and any letters to Lorna are also missing.

He clicked on pay days, picnic races, the CO, privates, officers, sergeants, the battalion band, Christmas comforts, men cleaning sand and grime from clothes or themselves, pistol practice and people writing home. For the rural volunteers, and the city blokes who made up the numbers, he captured their first overseas travel, many exotic scenes, with the Holy Places of Jerusalem of especial appeal to church-going troops. Here's his tent with photos of Lorna prominent … and Major Harry Tasker, second in command, gazing on the doll he had bought for his daughter Celia.

If you were careless (or feeling very creative) it was possible to take a double exposure. Here are overlapping spectral soldiers on route marches, an eerie recollection of Will Longstaff's hugely popular Great War painting *Menin Gate at Midnight*, with ghostly soldiers at Ypres.

His captions record the expected irreverent, traditional or up-to-date Diggers' nicknames: Tich the batman, Torchy Maguire, Dusty Rhodes, Cocky Walpole, even a contemporary Balbo Maxwell-Wright, named after the fascist Italian flying ace, Italo Balbo, who served as Mussolini's Marshal of the Air Force.

He judged, as an officer must: the images include an 'excellent' comment on soldiers, but only two criticisms noted, two men dismissed as 'no hopers' and another 'not worth a pinch of salt in spite of his stripe'.

Don't look for corpses. There is only one 'action shot' of the enemy – Italians surrendering. He later recorded the vanquished behind the wire of the Geneifa prisoner-of-war camp near Cairo.

Dad poses beside a mate in a forward post: his caption is *G.G. Anderson KIA July 1942* (Killed In Action). That's Graham Anderson, once a salesman in the Melbourne suburb of Prahran, dead at Tel El Eisa. Other shots show colleagues visiting cemeteries.

Even the official photographers found almost nothing in the way of ground combat opportunities, as the action was largely at night. (They were also not above some creative licence to liven up a photograph.)

There's little in my father's images to suggest the chaos, panic, manic action, stoicism, exhaustion and perhaps exultation of these comrades defending the weapon pits Australians had earlier captured from Italian troops: no hint of what today we call PTSD, or the haunting look sometimes described as the thousand-yard stare.

And while the D-Day beach scenes of *Saving Private Ryan* may offer a brutal glimpse of war's realities, no Dolby sound system could capture – nor an audience endure – battle's sound assault on the nervous system.

They're history now, these men who did their duty, opposing equally loyal men in the near-empty wastes of Libya. While there's no such thing as a 'Good War', incidents of what my generation know as the weasel words 'collateral damage' were infrequent. The conventions of war were usually honoured: those who surrendered were likely to survive and reach a POW camp. Land mines, however, caused civilian deaths long after the soldiers had departed, and are still a threat.

Those members of the 2/24th who went on to fight in the jungles of the Pacific looked back on Tobruk as a place where enemies were respected.

The battalion, originally Victorian, broadened to include soldiers from all States. The few survivors are well into their 90s but the battalion is still represented at various Anzac Day services.

Top
Lt John Rosel's medals and an ash tray he souvenired from Shepheard's Hotel, Cairo, rest on a 'Tobruk May 1941' page from his album.

Bottom
'On bivouac'
The spectral soldiers on this double exposure recall the ghostly legions in Will Longstaff's popular 1927 painting *Menin Gate at Midnight*.
Rear: *This would have been a beaut but Ken P looks like two on one. On the way home from the Bivy. I'm third from the front on the right.*

'G.G. Anderson, Freddie Geale, Ian Malloch'
Post S10 at Tobruk: Captain Graham Grantham Anderson was killed in action in July 1942. The former salesman from Prahran, Melbourne, is buried at the El Alamein war cemetery. His father, Major G.G. Anderson, was apparently in charge of No 51 General Hospital at Etaples in France when he died suddenly just eight days before the end of the Great War. Father and son were both only children.

Note on the Captions

The album caption (if any) is in quotes;
Any of John's notes on the back of photographs are *italicised*;
Other texts in plain type.

THE PHOTOGRAPHER

PEACETIME PRELUDE

There is irony in John Rosel's combat against the Germans of General Erwin Rommel's Afrika Korps. Growing up in Melbourne, my generation received only vague answers (deliberately so?), to their infrequent questions about the origins of a name unusual in Australia. There was talk of Alsace-Lorraine, the French territories seized by Germany after the Franco-Prussian war in 1871. But not until my brother Gerald and I launched family research in the 1970s did we confirm our German origin, unearthing an 1841 certification of birth from a Lutheran pastor at the small village of Schneeren, outside Hannover in Lower Saxony.

Genealogical detective work revealed that John's grandfather, Friedrich August Karl Ludwig Rößel ('Louis') – along with brothers Augustus and Henry, and sister Julia – had migrated to Victoria from 1854, joining thousands of Germans headed for the goldfields. When the older boys arrived at Melbourne on the good ship *San Francisco* from Hamburg in 1854, their surnames were anglicised as Rosel on the passenger manifests. Christian names were similarly treated.

By way of the Lauriston and Maindample goldfields and Echuca, Louis settled in the tiny Wimmera town of Natimuk, west of Horsham, where he bought the Natimuk Hotel in 1885. This was one of the villages first settled by families of German descent who had trekked in two generations from the Barossa Valley. The German names of some small Wimmera towns were changed in the wake of anti-German hysteria in 1914 which saw some 4,500 'enemy aliens' and Australians of German descent interned.

German names dominate Natimuk streets, among them Gladigau, Sudholz, Luhne, Lange, Schmidt, Schurmann, and Werner.

Thousands of Australians of German descent joined the First AIF. For anyone who might question their loyalty, a prominent inscription on the grave of William Schunke (died June 1916, aged 61) in the windswept Natimuk cemetery offers a poignant, perhaps pointed, memorial:

Also Our Soldier Sons.
Pte Arthur Schunke
Died of wounds.
Aged 31 years
And
Sgt Edwin Schunke
Killed in action in France.
Aged 24 years.
Greater love hath no man than this.

William Arthur Schunke survived an earlier wound (and mumps and measles while overseas) before dying of wounds on 12 October 1917.

Thirteen days later, his brother Edwin Ernest Schunke (who had already been wounded twice) was killed in action. They are buried in Belgium.

Mrs Anna Maria Schunke had been widowed, and lost two sons, over 16 months. She lived to 91. (In March 1916, five members of the Natimuk Recruiting Committee had written to the Commandant, 3rd Military District: 'We the undersigned can vouch for the loyalty of William Arthur Schunke of Natimuk.')

* * *

John Sefton Rosel was born in 1917 at Natimuk on January 26, a day not yet nationally celebrated as Australia Day. This was a dread year in our national history, with the Gallipoli losses of 1915 eclipsed by the 23,000 Australian casualties in six weeks of the Somme offensive in 1916, followed by Passchendaele in 1917. The nation was riven by the conscription debates and religious bigotry.

We discovered a tradition of Rosel military service for their adopted country. When updating the family history we were astonished to find – courtesy of the National Library's superb online Trove searchable index of almost all Australian city and country papers, Government Gazettes and other sources – that only eight years after his arrival in Australia, the oldest Rosel migrant, Augustus, was mentioned in *Government Gazette 86* of August 1866: 'His Excellency the Officer administering the Government, has been pleased to appoint AUGUSTUS. F.C. ROSEL, esquire, to be Lieutenant in the 2nd Castlemaine Rifle Corps.' The Kyneton businessman, a veteran of compulsory military service in Germany, later joined the Kyneton Volunteer Rifles, winning marksmanship prizes at Challenge Cup matches in 1868.

Such are the minutiae available through Trove, a national treasure. It helped that we had an unusual name: searching simply for ROSEL in 2014 yielded 697 pages with 13,937 Rosel entries to be winnowed, many being duplicated ads for family hotels and gold mining shares and equipment. If you are a Smith or Nguyen or Rossi or Pappas, or a similar common name, be prepared for a monstrous search task. Trove also yielded mentions of the next Rosel military volunteer. Augustus' grandson Fred left the Echuca Post Office to enlist underage in the Great War. He was badly wounded on the Western Front just seven weeks before the war ended.

If you fancy coincidence, and can recall the numbing climax to Peter Weir's 1981 film *Gallipoli*, where the prewar champion runner, Archy Hamilton, sprints to his death at The Nek …

In 1913, Fred Rosel earned a silver cup for winning the Old Boys' Race at the Echuca High School sports. His sprinting prowess proved no defence against shellfire and machine guns when his 46th Battalion attacked on 18 September 1918. His postwar letter to Colonel F. Hilbright of the 14th Battalion explained: 'At the entanglements I lost all interest, my mates took care of me. History says [he is quoting historian Charles Bean] the extraordinarily daring attack … resulted in an achievement to which there were few parallels on the Western Front.' He also praised 'the Spirit of Anzac … loyalty was demanded not asked, regardless of the price. We knew our mates would not let us down, if we fell, we knew they would be back after they had dealt with the enemy. If we had a chance they would get us out, if not they would end our suffering …'

Badly damaged in body and spirit, Fred survived just short of 50 years after his wounding. A telephone lineman, working to help returned soldiers, he found some comfort in drink and gambling. His Old Boys Race cup gleams against the grey technology on my desk.

* * *

My father was only nine when the comfortable village life at Natimuk ended in tragedy with his father's suicide. His mother Molly took the four children to Melbourne, where John and his brother Allan attended Xavier College. While only 178 cm tall, John was stocky, tough, a good all-round sportsman who shared the ruck work when Xavier won a rare Public Schools premiership in 1933. He also rowed. He shone both in the explosive, individual aggression of the ruck, and the synchronised teamwork of rowing. He was building a reputation as calm, unflappable, qualities to be tested in combat.

In the middle of the Depression, aged 17, he left school (he completed Year 11) after the first term of 1934 and walked the streets with his mother seeking a job. A stroke of luck at last: a case of 'who you know'. His sister Sheila recalled that an old family friend from Natimuk days returned from London as General Manager of the National Bank. John's mother had lost a lot of money after accepting bad investment advice from a rural National manager. As an apparent gesture of compensation, John started as a National Bank probationer at Elsternwick on 18 July 1934.

Family photos from the 1930s show a handsome, smiling young man, often with a cigarette at a jaunty angle. His friends photographed on Mornington Peninsula beaches and at Manresa, the Hawthorn parish tennis courts, had few illusions about war, unlike those who rushed to volunteer in 1914. Community losses from the Great War – 60,000 Australian dead – and daily sights of TPIs (Totally and Permanently Incapacitated pensioners), were reinforced by the flood of war poetry, memoirs (notably Robert Graves' *Goodbye To All That*, and Ernst Junger's *Storm of Steel*) and antiwar books like Erich Maria Remarque's *All Quiet On The Western Front* (filmed in 1930), Henri Barbusse's *Under Fire*, and the Australian novelist Frederic Manning's *The Middle Parts of Fortune* (also *Her Privates We*), sometimes cited as the greatest novel of the war.

In the last years of peace, he met Lorna Knowles, daughter of a Carlton monumental mason, at Manresa. She was a State public servant.

When the Militia – the Army Reserve – was doubled in size from 1938 in response to the looming war, John Rosel responded by serving with the 6th Militia Battalion for a year. By mid-1939 there were more than 80,000 serving. There was a serious shortage of equipment.

In 1940 he enlisted in the 2nd AIF: his medical exam on 14 May noted 'fresh complexion, blue eyes, fair hair, height 5 ft 10¼ inches [178.4 cm], weight 171 lb [77.5 kg].' He was appointed Lieutenant on 1 August 1940 and joined the 2/24th Battalion on 26 August.

* * *

This book is partly the tale of two Diggers, John Rosel, and David Henry ('Harry') Frazer of Swan Hill on the Murray River in northern Victoria. Prewar, Harry was busy in his family's hardware store and funeral director's business. Harry was no stranger to death – but not yet on an industrial scale.

Coming from a very musical family, he played cornet and trumpet in a Swan Hill band.

Aged 26 when war broke out, the battalion bandsman was to fight in John Rosel's platoon in the most violent and desperate circumstances at Tobruk.

The girl he left behind: John Rosel and Lorna Knowles, c.1940.

MAKING SOLDIERS

'MY CHAPS'

Midwinter, the rural city of Wangaratta in northeast Victoria. Men of the 2/24th Battalion, raised at Caulfield on 1 July 1940, gathered at the Showgrounds for training. After some reorganisation, the old sweats and the new volunteers of the 2/24th were to serve with the 9th Australian Division, under the command of 26th Brigade Headquarters. Their battalion's Commanding Officer was Lt Colonel Allan Spowers.

The people of Wangaratta adopted the battalion and gave it the honorary title of 'Wangaratta's Own'.

Sergeant Sam Fry of 'A' Company described conditions at Wangaratta in the battalion history:

> By this time – the middle of September – we had really become used to conditions in camp. The dreadful damp of the cattle stalls had cleared up, we had all recovered from 'Pucka throat' [Puckapunyal was a large Army

> base in central Victoria] and hot showers were at last available. Our band took shape and was to gain much renown in the Middle East.

(One of the band members was Private Harry Frazer, whose letters home from Tobruk were to provide a lively and intimate account of the siege. More later.)

On 27 September the battalion tramped past the citizens of Wangaratta to start a four-day march to new, if spartan huts at Bonegilla. Diggers are never far from a practical joke. Sergeant Alan Macfarlane, deputised to carry the 14 ft pennant presented by the town, couldn't understand why the honour was so tiring. Until he woke up that somebody had added two bricks to his pack.

Diggers were also not afraid of a little larceny, call it souveniring, scrounging, improvisation, whatever. At the bivouac at Rising Sun Creek, Sgt Fry recalled 'an incident with a small pig, an irate farmer and a more irate C.O. [Commanding Officer]. That pig was really expensive meat.'

At Bonegilla, Lt Rosel picked up his camera to record the basic barracks, unlined huts which kept out only rain and wind, and the men who made the most of them. Here is his platoon (*my chaps* pencilled on the back), and soldiers sprawled by the roadside during a route march.

The battalion's history was to be edited by Major R.P. (Bob) Serle, a former CMF officer, and the only officer who took part in the four campaigns in which the battalion fought. He wrote the story up to the end of the siege, and this book could not have been written without extensive quoting from his text.

In his introduction he noted that

> not only did a very powerful divisional feeling grow over the years, but an even greater pride in the ability and reputation of the battalion as a whole ... its traditions sprang naturally from the deeds of the First AIF.

Some older soldiers had served in the Great War, creating the legends, and some myths, of the First AIF.

Some of the older volunteers might have seen Will Dyson's famously prescient cartoon in London's *Daily Mail* of 13 May 1919. The former Australian official war artist sketched four of the peacemakers leaving the Palace of Versailles. Hidden by a pillar is a crying child labelled 'Class of 1940' – the cohort of young men who would then come of age for military service. The French Prime Minister, Georges Clemenceau ('The Tiger') is speaking – the caption reads: 'The Tiger: Curious! Methinks I seem to hear a child weeping.'

The young Australians at Bonegilla, literally Dyson's Class of 1940, had been stunned by the ease with which the Germans crushed France in a few weeks in May 1940.

Only eight days before the battalion was born, a vengeful Hitler had ordered the surrender to be signed in the same railway carriage at Compiegne in which the German Government signed the Great War Armistice on 11 November 1918.

Germany had bequeathed the world a new word – 'blitzkrieg', lightning war.

There was definitely the sense of 'second time around'. Out from the armouries and quartermasters' stores were resurrected the weapons, uniforms and kit of the Great War; especially the iconic .303 rifle, the SMLE (Short Magazine Lee Enfield) which was to serve British units for the first half of the 20th century. For the left-handed Lt Rosel, the bolt which closed on the right side made for awkward rapid fire.

Some would master the Vickers machine gun: there were mortars and grenades …

And, eventually, an excellent new light machinegun to replace the obsolete Lewis gun. The Diggers had to wait to receive the Bren, based on a Czech design. Its forward-curving upper magazine identified it in all arenas of WWII combat and beyond.

To tackle the Panzers, they had Boyes anti-tank rifles, a scaled-up rifle with a massive kick, dangerous only to lightly armoured targets. Nobody clamoured for a second firing.

(They did not know it, but the year before, a young Wollongong inventor, Evelyn Owen, had designed a submachine gun which would be refined as the Owen gun. In service from 1943, it was used by the battalion in the Pacific, where it was famed for continuing to fire in atrocious conditions.)

Colonel Spowers was a demon for hard marching, a basic attribute of fitness essential to turn civilians into soldiers. His mantra was 'As ye train so shall ye fight' and he had officers roaming the back roads seeking new routes.

The men had to break in Army boots, just as their leaders had to break them in to the necessary rituals of immediate obedience to orders, initially expressed through 'square bashing' or parade, refined in choreographed 'battle drills' with whatever supporting arms were available. Australia lacked anything to match the panzers whose mobility and central command had humbled France.

Individual initiative was prized, but recklessness never condoned.

The men revived WWI marching songs (the popular tune *Tipperary* was one of few fit for public consumption) and borrowed new ones. ('We'll hang out our washing on the Siegfried Line.')

Lt Rosel and his fellow officers urged them along, halting for a ten-minute break every hour. For many, the cigarettes came out – 'smoko'.

Serle recalled:

> So there was developed the spirit of the battalion – hard work, the striving to attain the standard set, comradeship, co-operation and tolerance which developed between all ranks as we came to know each other ... The original civilians became soldiers, perhaps not the pattern of soldier which is distinguished by the outward signs of military showmanship, but very definitely soldiers by the standards of the AIF.

While the usual traditions of addressing officers and NCOs by their ranks was followed – and the use of 'sir' to officers – off parade, officers and NCOs would address individuals only by their rank and surname, or their Christian name. 'For some reason the use of surnames without prefix was resented by the addressee,' Serle wrote. 'There must be some connotation of master and servant attaching to this practice which offends the spirit of Australian democracy, and we never employed it.'

Certainly there are no salutes recorded by Lt Rosel's camera.

The officers emphasised personal hygiene.

> In later years we were amazed to see allied troops who apparently could not cope with difficult conditions, and seemed to imagine that to be dirty and bearded was the mark of a tough soldier.

The equipment position was not good. Rifle companies had barely sighted a Bren, let alone trained with one. Submachine guns were unknown until a few Tommy guns (Thompson guns, famous as the Chicago gangsters' weapon) were issued in Tobruk.

All Army transport vehicles were horse-drawn except for some civilian trucks called in for Army service. 'It was a sad commentary on the state of preparedness for war in Australia nearly one year after its commencement,' Serle noted: 'Not until 1942 did our supply of weapons become adequate.'

Sgt Fry:

> The continued hectic training was tempered with the feeling that 'It couldn't be long now' and our hopes were raised in mid-October when the orders for the fateful 'Final Leave' were issued. All but a few key personnel left camp on 18 October for a final glorious week.

There were emotional farewells at Spencer St. station in Melbourne on 25 October as soldiers 'in all stages of seriousness and sobriety' said their goodbyes. 'That is, except the 150 or so who had decided that a week wasn't enough. Most of them came good, even it was at the boatside some weeks later.'

The battalion received its number – 408 – and colours, brown-green and brown.

There were embarkation rolls, immunizations and vaccinations, official photographs: 'All we had to do now was to wait, to listen to rumours, and to spread them.'

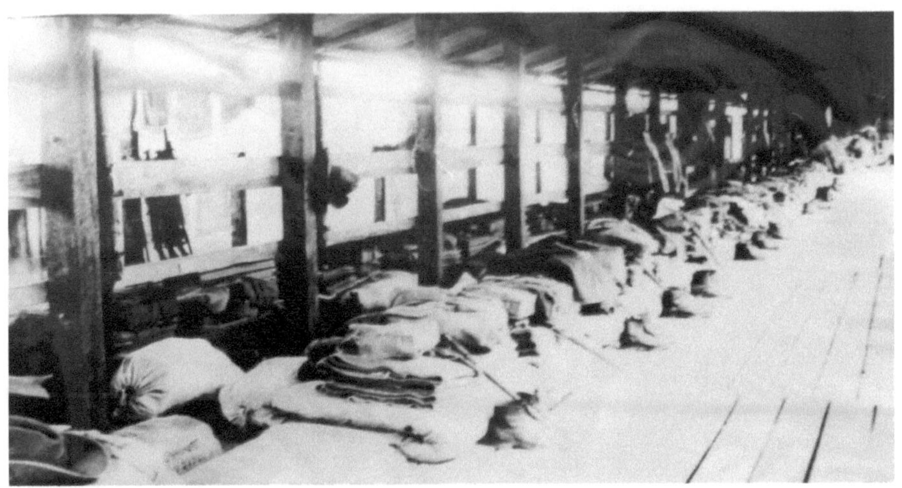

Top

'The dreadful damp of the cattle stalls'
Lt Alan Macfarlane's photo of Diggers' bedding, boots, hats, rifles, and kitbags at their Wangaratta Showgrounds sleeping quarters in 1940.
Did any recall lines from *Anthem for Doomed Youth,* Wilfred Owen's famous Great War poem: *What passing bells for these who die as cattle? / Only the monstrous anger of the guns ...*

Bottom

Diggers' rest: a ten-minute break on a route march out of Bonegilla, 1940.
Rear: *Frank, Ev and Ken on way out.*

Top

'5.30am'

First cigarette of the day for Lt John Rosel on bivouac outside Bonegilla, 1940.

Bottom

'L[ieutenant] Rosel, C[aptain] Baillieu, C[aptain] Budge, L[ieutenant] Shelton, L[ieutenant] Kelly'

Pictured in front of a Bonegilla hut. John Shelton would die in Tobruk, driving an open Bren Gun carrier struck by a German tank shell during the Battle of the Salient.

TRANSIT TO WAR

'TED' AND THE TOURISTS

The 2/24th embarked on HMT *Strathmore*, a P&O ocean liner turned troopship, their home for the next few weeks.

'The comparative luxury and calm of shipboard life was a big change,' Sgt Fry wrote. 'Most of us settled in cabins fitted with additional wooden bunks.' (John Rosel and the rest of 'C' Company slept in hammocks, once they got used to them.)

After a welcome break in Perth, *Strathmore* sailed on. Fry recorded 'a most uncomfortable outbreak of enteritis [inflammation of the intestine, usually accompanied by diarrhoea] and several hundred answered the call for sick parade, if they could make it.'

Strathmore docked at Colombo in Ceylon (Sri Lanka) and the troops were armed with rupees for a day's leave. For many it was the first sight of a foreign land – although some had heard the tales of the First AIF which preceded them in 1914. Sgt Fry:

> Our eyes, ears and noses were assailed by new and strange sights, sounds and smells. Many fell victim to crafty conmen, others toured the city in rickshaws, while a thoughtful few undertook a brief trip to the ancient capital of Kandy.

Lt Rosel's camera ran hot. In checking the backs of some of the Colombo photos we made a touching family discovery – he'd concluded some of his notes to Lorna (aka Pet or Darling) as Ted, or Ole' Ted. We could only think their nickname was short for Teddy Bear, although it was difficult to imagine our father as cuddly.

Strathmore sailed on, and air-raid precautions commenced. On 12 December *Strathmore* entered the Red Sea at dusk … 'It was obvious from preparations being made that our journey was almost at an end.'

Lt O'Day of the 2/14th Battalion boarded at Suez with plans of their future movements, and lurid tales of the locals: 'Many were the tales he told us of the 'perils' of life in Palestine and the craftiness of the "wogs" as we sailed into the canal, excitedly watching the various scenes. The Arabs at their prayers. The donkeys and camels, the tiny patches of cultivation.'

They disembarked at the canal port of Kantara on 17 December

> but there were to be none of the fleshpots of Egypt for us. We moved on to the desert side of the canal and after a breakfast of bread and eggs – 'the smallest, hardest and most unpleasant ever tasted' – we passed the day with dirty-nosed Arab youngsters who spoke to us in what they thought was Australian … it was obvious that the 6th Division had been here before us.

The troop train crossed miles of rolling sand through the Sinai Desert, which gave way to pockets of vegetation near the frontier, and then came their first city, Gaza. By late afternoon they were in their camp at Dimra at the Australian Base Area in Palestine, some 15 km north of Gaza at the base of the Gaza Ridge. There was a sobering reminder of war with spent cartridge cases and pieces of shell from the WWI battles here between the Australian Light Horse and the Turks.

> We knew nothing of the exciting events unfolding in the desert, of Western Desert Force's outstanding victory at Sidi Barrani against the Italians. The 2nd AIF was about to go into action for the first time and the 6th Division was to prove itself at Bardia and Tobruk.

Brens at last appeared in useful numbers, and they learned to dislike the Boyes anti-tank rifle: 'Scarcity of ammunition restricted its firing to one round per man, quite sufficient to tickle up the shoulder blade, for the recoil was intense on firing.'

There were many interesting sights. Women doing heavy manual work on the roads. Donkeys, camels, hordes of curious children, veiled women.

Rainstorms forced at least half of the tents to be shifted to higher ground. On Christmas Eve, hampers from the Australian Comforts Fund were distributed – welcome scarves, balaclavas, toilet gear and other blessings. Then Christmas Dinner when, by tradition, officers served the troops.

They sampled desert conditions with a full day's exercise in the dunes and on the beach before New Year. 'Sand and sun are normally a pleasant combination, but with heavy boots, a loaded pack and 70-degree slopes, a very weary battalion straggled into camp.' The battalion's first casualty, Private Lord, drowned at Tel Aviv beach while on leave.

News of the 6th Division's successful operation at Bardia added purpose to training – 'Who knew how soon it would be our turn?' The usual route march was twenty to twenty-five miles (32 to 40 km). They wondered who invented 'goldfish' (tinned herring):

> Hot and sweaty, with aching feet and dry throats, a picnic lunch of 'goldfish' and oranges was hardly the most appetising fare, but in a few months many would have given anything for just one tin of the despised 'goldfish' so cheerfully discarded then.

Sgt E.A. Fishlock died as the result of an operation and was buried in Gaza War Cemetery near many Australian casualties of WWI.

They were encouraged to hear of Tobruk falling on 22 January 1941, with 25,000 Italian prisoners.

February brought range training at Jaffa. Those with Biblical knowledge had heard of Askelon, as they marched past ancient ruins there.

Gradually order grew out of the chaos of the early battalion exercises. Officers and men worked hard and played hard.

First big leave, for 400 men, destination Jerusalem: 'Unknown to us, this was to be the last day or freedom for many months – even years – and we enjoyed it.'

Those unfit for infantry work on active service were transferred to the guard battalion.

Top

'John, Colombo'

Rear: *The old chap told us he owned the island. Personally he looked as if he was nearly broke. Love Teddy xo*

The two lads on either side are the waiters from the hotel where we had lunch at Kandy. That was a great but hurried trip. How's the look on the lad in the shafts.

Bottom

'Xmas comforts 1940'

Un-boxing day: opening comforts hampers, Palestine.

Left

'Church of the Nativity, Bethlehem'
Lt Rosel second from left.
Rear: *This one the guide took Pet. Remember me saying that the old doors had been sealed with only a small hole to get through – well here it is.*

Below

'Cocky Walpole running his book'
At the donkey races, Christmas 1940.
Rear: … *Cocky has the white singlet on.*

Top
Bayonet course training, Palestine.

Bottom
Palestine, 21 March 1941. The 2/24th Band won a Divisional band contest. Private Harry Frazer (fourth from right) was one of four members from Swan Hill. Five weeks later the bandsmen were to swap musical instruments for rifles in the defence of Tobruk. (From his family album.)

Top

'!'

John Rosel enjoys a tub bath.

Rear: *Whoopee. Nothing's going to dampen my spirits. What about yours Darling?*

Bottom

'Dead Sea'

Rear: *Peter Hayman kneeling,* [from left] *Sgt Maj Morrison, John E and Ole Ted.*

Peter Hayman MC was to die at El Alamein.

The officers received a sobering presentation on the 6th Division's capture of Tobruk.

> Never even having seen our artillery fire a shell up to this point, we realised how much we had to learn. Nor had we seen a tank or anti-tank gun in Palestine. Unfortunately, our Divisional artillery had no guns with which to work at this stage and we were all due to learn the hard way, such was our innocence of the hard facts of war in the desert. Nevertheless by the middle of March, under the determined guidance of the CO, all those who could not stand up to the hardening process had been weeded out and the battalion consisted of some nine hundred young men in the prime of physical and mental condition … the real show now commenced.

'THE BENGHAZI HANDICAP'

10 MARCH–10 APRIL 1941

The battalion went by truck to Gazala, west of Tobruk. The Diggers were learning how to live in the open desert: each man had a groundsheet, two blankets and a greatcoat, and they scrounged wreckage on Gazala airstrip for anything that would make a roof over a hastily excavated dugout.

They tried their first night movements on the featureless desert, with the Pole Star to indicate north. If you were lucky you had a luminous oil compass. There were firing exercises with captured Italian ammunition and weapons, and lectures on the Italian 'pillbox' hand grenade and box-type anti-tank mine.

On March 26 the battalion moved west in Chevrolet trucks into the 'Green Belt' of Cyrenaica, camping at Tocra on the second night. They were responsible for guarding the escarpment from Tocra to Tolmeta.

‘Our attitude towards any useful article was positively miserly,’ the history says.

> Since coming up the desert we were developing as first-class scroungers and were making use of any unconsidered trifles that came our way. We were also developing our ability to salvage, repair and incorporate those articles into our daily way of life in lieu of items on our equipment table which never seemed to reach us.

General Rommel’s Afrika Korps then overwhelmed the 2nd British Armoured Division, and moved towards the vital Suez Canal. ‘From this day on until we reached Tobruk nine days later, the fog of war descended and enveloped us completely,’ Bob Serle wrote.

The Germans’ two-pronged attack was daring, given their supply position. Withdrawal behind a major anti-tank obstacle became inevitable.

A retreat began. Trucks were grossly overloaded and surplus gear was destroyed. The battalion travelled eastward during the night, past burning dumps: bridges were blown behind the retreating troops.

Such was the confusion that British Generals Philip Neame and Richard O’Connor took the wrong road and were captured by the Germans.

During the retreat commanders and staff officers often personally handled the traffic.

With armour depleted, it was obvious that the infantry had to withdraw behind the Tobruk perimeter to withstand a tank attack. Tobruk had to be held as there was not enough transport to move troops beyond. It held the defenders’ main supply of food and ammunition (brought up by sea) and water was not an issue.

As my father was often to say – a colourful euphemism in the face of awesome confusion – it was 'a real schemozzle.' (He would never use the universal vulgar alternative if kids were around.)

Serle concluded:

> So ended the last lap of the famous 'Benghazi Handicap'. The battalion had been fortunate to arrive back without casualties and with all its weapons and vehicles intact … we were disgusted at being pushed around, always falling back before we could use our own weapons against the enemy, but determined that one day soon we would hit back.
>
> On the German side, their initiative and daring received full marks from us.

Last Man from Benghazi?

Diggers always ready to laugh at themselves quickly dubbed the rapid Allied retreat 'The Benghazi Handicap'.

According to *The Furphy Flyer in Mufti** (civilian clothes), the postwar newsletter of the 2/24th Battalion, Lt John Rosel and a medic may have been the last Diggers out of town on that memorable evacuation.

Its November 1987 issue included a story by diver Stan Aitken suggesting the fluidity of desert warfare:

---

* *The Furphy Flyer* was the battalion newssheet produced in Tobruk during the siege. 'Furphy' was colloquial speech for rumour, named for the mobile water carts made by Furphy of Shepparton, which attracted gossiping soldiers. 'Furphy' is one of those endearing and enduring survivors of uniquely Australian slang.

> Whilst I was at Tocra Pass I was ordered to take our RMO [Regimental Medical Officer – Captain T.E. (Guy) Robertson] and Lieut Rosel on a dash to Benghazi in search of medical supplies – at that stage the Africa Korps had just appeared in North Africa. En route we were frequently stopped by the notorious Red Caps [military police] urging us to go back, but the doc pulled rank and I reluctantly pressed on.
>
> Arriving in Benghazi it became very obvious that the famous town was about to change hands, so after picking up a few bits and pieces we dashed back to Tocra. I would imagine that even today the time I took to get from Benghazi to Tocra may still be a record.

Lt Rosel, being a dutiful photographer, kept firing off pictures of burning dumps as they retreated. They are among his images passed to the Australian War Memorial.

'Benghazi. The withdrawal'
April 1941: Lt Rosel and the Regimental Medical Officer made a last-minute dash to Benghazi chasing medical supplies as the Afrika Korps closed in.
Rear: *Benghazi dumps burning.*

COMBAT IN TOBRUK

'THE POOR OLD 24TH'

Early days, 10–29 April 1941

The battalion was about to be severely tested. As the noted Australian war correspondent Chester Wilmot summarised in *Tobruk*, the Australians were short of training, equipment and experience.

> Most of them and many of the British troops had come through a week of dispiriting, bewildering withdrawal … compared with the enemy, the garrison had but a handful of tanks and aircraft.

Our father – schoolboy sportsman, bank officer and citizen soldier – had responsibility for 30 men.

Sixty years after the battle, Alan Macfarlane, once one of his fellow Lieutenants and long a President of the 2/24th Battalion Association, characterised him as

> a bloody good soldier, a great bloke, rarely without a smile on his face. When he smiled he put his whole face into it. The only thing we argued about was religion. He and John Christie were the only ones who didn't drink beer. We called them the sober twins.
>
> He was an excellent platoon commander, fastidious in his operation, and he nurtured his men well.

Sobriety would help in the face of the Afrika Korps.

He embodied that often praised, if not always honoured Australian trait, A Fair Go. His children would later imagine him sharing around the platoon's duties, whether ordering unpleasant tasks – latrine hygiene, anyone? – or choosing men for the hazardous night patrols claimed to give an edge to the Australians.

The Germans had followed up the withdrawal quickly, and on the first day of the siege started the shelling which was to characterise the life of forward battalions.

There were some 35,000 troops within the perimeter, including 14,000 Australians. Soldiers worked hard to clear the former Italian positions and collect many Italian weapons to boost their own defences. Although the Italian guns usually lacked their sights, amateur if enthusiastic Diggers formed the Bush Artillery, contributing usefully to the defence. They fired away huge stores of captured ammunition with volume partly compensating for rough-as-guts accuracy.

The situation at this time was fluid – 'C' Company fired some of their first shots in anger when Lt Rosel fired his Bren at long range at a motor cyclist across a wadi (valley or gully).

This was hard manual labour:

> Fire positions for weapons had to be built; ammunition had to be manhandled close to the weapons; reserve rations had to be collected; and sandbags, wire and tools brought up. Endless miles of Italian cable were picked up from the ground and strung out again to provide the basis of our own signal system … concrete posts were habitable but we were not too happy about occupying some stone sangars standing out well above ground level.

Hard rock was usually less than 600 mm down, where it was not exposed by erosion. While the Italian engineers had used explosives to blast the rock when making concrete weapon pits, dugouts and anti-tank ditches, the Australians had only picks and shovels to remove debris and improve defences.

(Sharing the shovel work, Lt Rosel would not have known that his German grandfather Louis had successfully hacked out gold-bearing quartz deep below Lauriston in 1865. Had he known, we reckon he would have laughed; he was always one to make the best of a situation. Truly, a Digger – even if he was photographed resting on his shovel.)

Extracts from Major Len Fell's diary for the next ten days give an idea of the problems facing the Australians awaiting a well-equipped and trained enemy:

> Our own equipment was far from adequate … men not on duty lived in sangars, rations came up at night;

guard over pumping station, wells in wadis; fleas; dog fights; noise of planes at night; gunfire at night on Derna road; patrols; sea beaches and bathing; killing of goats and sheep for food; no possible chance against AFVs [armoured fighting vehicles]; no field glasses or submachine guns; communications – shortage of DRs (motorcycle Despatch Riders), transport, guns, grenades, compasses. Use of LMG [light machinegun] for AA [anti-aircraft] – age of officers; necessity for training to do with little sleep and take it when you can get it; ... vital necessity for good NCOs and those NCOs suitable for training often are not suitable for war – I.O. [Intelligence Officer] useless if not good; tactical and other schools must apply lessons to type of warfare and country; information on working with tanks, behind barrages, loading of vehicles, Geneva Convention, – building of sangars, realism in training, don't allow camp routine to interfere with training.

The Australians were given a little time to address a formidable list of concerns as Rommel built up his forces at the end of a long supply line.

He attacked the 20th Brigade front on Good Friday – 11 April – and Easter Monday, but was repulsed. The Germans realised a full-scale attack would be needed. In the meantime, there were minor attacks, and Australian patrolling: Italian prisoners were taken.

The soldiers enjoyed dogfights between enemy aircraft and the few Hurricanes still flying from Tobruk. The band, which had played on occasions in the wadi near the sea, was broken up and its members sent to rifle companies (mostly as stretcher-bearers). Enter Harry Frazer as rifleman.

The battalion moved to the Red Line – the forward defences – on April 28th and 29th. At 1.30pm on April 29 an enemy aircraft machinegunned the Battalion Headquarters and 'C' Company headquarters, killing one man and wounding four.

Five Stukas dive-bombed 'B' Company; before dusk German armoured cars and infantry were fired on by 'A' Company.

Serle wrote:

> This activity, including ranging by artillery, was in fact a clear indication that Point 209 had been selected as the first objective of a set-piece attack ... The events of the next three days will never be forgotten by those who participated … up to this time we had not been attacked at close quarters by the full-scale Panzer drive that had carried all before it in Poland, France and Cyrenaica. Now Tobruk was to be given the full treatment – Stukas, artillery, tanks, then infantry, and on the German side all were confident of full success.

Above

'Stony sandy wadis'
Typical bare desert at Tobruk, June 1941. A wadi is a valley. The placement of the foreground rocks suggest they are the lip of a sangar, a rock breastwork defence, possibly part of Lt Rosel's Post S10.
Rear: *Tobruk is good sheep country like –*

Left

Real Diggers. Lt Rosel (left) and comrade (possibly Captain Ian Malloch) take a camera break while improving their Tobruk defence post, May 1941.

Top

'Italian prisoners surrendering'

Rear: *See them stringing in Pet – not a shot had been fired. Note one with white flag.*

Bottom

'Lunch Time'

Some 14 Platoon soldiers, in the front line, Tobruk. Lt John Rosel seated left. The two on the right appear well tanned.

'THE MAY SHOW'

'TRIUMPH AND TRAGEDY'

30 April–2 May 1941

The battalion would recall it as 'The May Show'.

> To Serle,
>
> the epic story of this struggle … was at one and the same time a tragedy and a triumph for the battalion. A tragedy because we lost so many of our members in one blow, a triumph because the German Afrika Korps received a major setback – so severe that it was forced to go over to the defensive and never again made a major attack on Tobruk throughout the period of the siege.

General Leslie Morshead's orders to forward battalions were clear:

> All positions are to be held at all costs. No withdrawals will be made. If positions are surrounded by the enemy, they are still to be held and will be relieved by counter-attack. Tanks should be allowed to pass through to be engaged by anti-tank and field guns in rear. Infantry following are to be engaged and defeated.

All very well. But the Germans had learned from their Easter failure, when Morshead's tactics had been successful.

Serle said the battalion's forward positions (the Red Line) 'became, in effect, an outpost line covering the main positions and by resisting so fiercely and for so long, completely upset the timing of the German attack.'

The violence of the assault, particularly the number of tanks, made infantry counter-attack impossible until nearly dusk on 1 May: too late for the Australians in the Red Line, who were largely overcome.

The main lesson, Serle emphasised, was that Australian governments should prepare better for war and not send their soldiers into battle without adequate weapons or essential equipment. For instance, the battalion did not have a single wireless set, and the recycled Italian signal wire for the field telephones was inevitably destroyed by shellfire. The last communications resort – runners – faced potentially lethal hazards.

'Lack of precise information hampered battalion, brigade and divisional commanders at all stages,' Serle added. 'It is probable that at brigade and divisional level the battle was fought "on the map" instead of by personal observation "on the ground".'

The concept of forward tactical command had not yet been

worked out, and there were no proper vehicles for commanders' reconnaissance.

> Due to lack of proper information at higher levels, we of the 2/24th battalion felt for some weeks after the May battle that we were definitely under a cloud, that the battalion was expected to have held its ground, as had the battalions of the 20th Brigade in the Easter attacks.
>
> By degrees this feeling was dispelled, as the strength of the enemy gradually became known, together with the extent of the damage and casualties inflicted on them. The attack … had not only failed to reach its objective, but half the attacking tanks had been knocked out of action by the end of the first day, with consequent dismay among the enemy High Command.

Brigadier Ray Tovell later summed up:

> On 1 May we lost some ground, but gained a great victory. The enemy concentrated on one sector, held by 2/24th Battalion, all the power of his tanks and dive bombers, but he failed to break through our deep defences.
>
> This battle was won primarily by the ordinary men and junior officers. It was won partly by the courage and tenacity of those in the front line who held out so well against an immense attack. They saw it coming, but they stuck to their posts. Many tanks got through but our troops held up the German infantry until they

> were literally blasted from their posts by tanks and flamethrowers.
>
> It was won partly by the gallantry of British gunners who stuck to their field and anti-tank guns through shelling, dive bombing and machine-gunning from the ground and the air. Their splendid shooting was a big factor in stopping the tanks, as captured German diaries show.

Serle wrote:

> The whole course of this battle illustrates once again the historical truth that handfuls of determined men can turn the tide, when the odds seem against any success, judged by material factors. It proved that plans of commanders, no matter how well thought out and executed, can be upset and negatived by the ordinary soldiers' stubborn resistance and the will to oppose the enemy's intentions.

* * *

While the details of the battle can be left to formal histories, an outline is helpful.

The three forward companies totalling around 300 soldiers manned 22 concrete posts stretched in an arc around the perimeter for around seven kilometres. 'A' company was protected by a minefield which arced just under a kilometre. General Morshead also ordered the laying of a tactical minefield stretching some 2.7 km behind the perimeter posts – this was one of the most important factors in stopping the tanks when the perimeter was breached. These mines, made in Egypt, could blow off a tank track but not injure the body of the Mark III and Mark IV tanks, or harm crews. Fortunately the Germans did not see – or ignored as a possible trap – the minefield gaps left for defenders' vehicles, which were marked by whitewashed stone cairns.

Most posts provided for two anti-tank guns in circular pits but lacked protected firing positions for machine-gunners or riflemen. Underground rooms were almost impregnable to bombing and shelling – accounting for the few casualties from these causes – but could be traps if defenders were forced from their ground-level positions. The posts were not connected by trenches and the average distance between them was 600–800 metres.

While the Italians had manned the concrete posts with 25 or more men, the Australians could muster only 10 or 15. The company frontages were far in excess of that considered defensible in later desert fighting: 'We had one man to each 25 yards of front!'

There was no time to construct new posts. There was barbed wire, and some Italian anti-tank and anti-personnel mines. Defences in this flat and usually featureless country were defensible by day, but it was nearly impossible for a vehicle to reach forward posts by day without being shelled. Supplies had to come by truck at night. There were frantic last-minute efforts to improve firing positions.

* * *

The attack started about 6.30pm with 40 Stukas dive-bombing perimeter posts and wire, causing no casualties, but compelling the signallers to repair telephone wires repeatedly cut by shelling.

At 8pm a heavy barrage came down along the perimeter selected for attack: no further reports were received from 'A' Company, while lines to 'D' and 'C' Companies worked intermittently for some hours.

> At 8.15pm there were reports of infantry approaching the forward posts … the enemy kept sending up coloured flares, indicating progress to his artillery … a feature of the barrage was the high velocity anti-tank shells emitting coloured tracer and ricocheting off the hard ground at strange and unpredictable angles. At this stage it was obvious that some perimeter penetration had been made behind the perimeter posts …

It was a world of confusion. Shelling caused a dust pall like a mist. There was little moonlight so it was difficult for a man to keep direction unless he had a track marked by stones or signal wire.

'In retrospect,' the history says, 'it is apparent that only a battalion counter-attack by experienced and properly-equipped troops who knew the ground could have evicted the enemy who had penetrated between our posts, and who were now digging in as best they could.'

Just after midnight there was a report that a relieving officer trying to get to 'A' Company had been fired on. 'A message from Lieutenant John Rosel, asking for help for "C" Company HQ, was also received …'

A MESSAGE FROM OUR FATHER

One of the most memorable and frequently cited documents from Tobruk is my father's field message sent back to HQ at the height of the battle in May.

First publicly reproduced in Serle's battalion history, it captures the pressure on troops under threat of being overwhelmed, as their neighbours had been.

In succinct military reportage in pages torn from his diary, John Rosel pencilled a grim picture.

In full, with explanations of some military abbreviations in square brackets:

> To D coy [2/23rd Battalion]
> From ISKA 14 [14 Platoon 2/24th Battalion]
>
> Received ammunition. No idea how 15 Pl [platoon] and COY HQ [Company Headquarters] are faring. 13

Pl lost forward section post S7. Enemy have occupied this post in strength. Also have light gun on ridge above this post making holding of this Pl area untenable. Enemy also have mortar in position on this ridge. Propose withdraw men from [posts] 8 and 9 and place them in 10 and 11a with my men. I have no communications with anyone outside. There appear to be some 2 hundred enemy across the wadi [valley] from S11. Came up in transport and are digging themselves in. Post S8 have 5 German prisoners, one being badly wounded. Wire in front of my position worthless. In 10 I have one Breda [Italian light machine gun], plenty of ammo, one Bren, 4,000 rounds. In 11a two Brens with total of 2,000 rounds. Post 11 – this includes your section – 1 Bren with 3,000, 1 Breda 3,000, 1 Iti [Italian] mortar with 300 bombs, only 50 ballistite rounds [for rifle grenades] 1 A/tk [anti-tank] rifle, 220 rounds. Another 2 days rations still on hand. Could you possibly contact ISKO (2/24Bn headquarters) and hand on this information. Hope you can understand this. Viva la Batallion [*sic*]. The position tonight is going to be very serious and if some reinforcements could be produced we would stand a fair chance. ISKO might know how our COY HQ + 15Pl stand. Here's hoping.

J. Rosel

15.40 [3.40pm]

Keeping one of your Brens.

'Captain G. I. Malloch MC'
Captain Ian Malloch of the 2/23rd Battalion led his company to determine the fate of Lt John Rosel's platoon.
Note mess tin and Bren gun.

Top

2/24th Battalion headquarters in a Tobruk cave. Harry Frazer, centre.
The signals switchboard at right.
Photograph from a Frazer family album.
Rear: *To Win, from Harry ... I think this is rather a good souvenir pet. It is a cave we were using up the desert. Jerry used to drop shells all round it and going to the cookhouse at meal times was always fun, wondering just where he would put the next one ... snap taken by a cobber of mine, Alan Devereaux.*

Bottom

'"Tich" Masters, batman'
Note the worn sole of his boot.
Rear: *Tich*

'Major Harry Tasker, O/C Training Battalion'
Rear: *Harry was so tickled with the doll he bought for his Celia, that I took his foto in the tent.*

Left
'Brown, Horan, Wright'
Rear: ... *excellent chaps* ...
Corporal Denis Horan died from injuries received when a wave swamped the deck of HMAS *Nizam*, carrying the battalion from Tobruk to Alexandria. Twenty soldiers were washed overboard, and six died.

Below
Captain Frank Budge. Probably a Beretta automatic captured from the Italians.

John Rosel took over command of 13 Platoon after the capture of Company HQ and as he had no communication with the Battalion HQ except through the wireless set of the British 51st Field Regiment, the remainder of 'C' Company came under command of the 2/23rd Battalion about 3pm on 1 May.

* * *

One incident among the confusion. From the history:

> At 6am our carriers moved forward towards 'B' Company, although it was not yet light … by 7am, the mist was lifting, and Lieutenant John Shelton volunteered to go forward to 'A' Company … observers saw his carrier drive down the Acroma road … the mist rolled down again … 20 minutes later a carrier was observed burning … tanks had knocked out his carrier … Shelton, who was driving was killed, but his foot jammed on the accelerator and his crew were able to turn the vehicle back; but they were then hit again and the petrol tank blew up … John Shelton had proved himself a courageous soldier and was the first of our officers to be killed in action.

* * *

The battle developed:

> By 7.30am the sun was up and the mist rapidly clearing; Suddenly, in dramatic fashion, just as if the curtain

> had lifted on a stage, the haze dispersed and enemy tanks were seen advancing towards 'B' Company and BHQ [battalion headquarters] … The I.O. [Intelligence Officer] sighted the tanks at 2500 metres through his binoculars … within a few minutes the count reached 80 … the Gunner F.O.O. [Forward Observing Officer] called for fire from his regiment, and from this time the 25-pounders behind us were continually in action.

By 8am the situation looked particularly grim. After coming through the gaps in the minefield, the enemy tanks had formed up by companies and were slowly advancing towards 'B' Company, under fire from the 51st Field Regiment.

The Intelligence Officer pointed out the approaching tanks to the commander of a British light tank, and shouted to him to do something about it, to which the reply was: 'They're ours!'

> The I.O.'s language then became most Australian and quite unprintable and the tank promptly backed off, and neither it nor any other British tank was seen from Battalion Headquarters for the rest of the day – not that anyone blamed them – the tank was an old tin-can, a Vickers Mark I, its armour not protection against anti-tank shells.

Serle continued:

> The tanks ran into our minefield and came to a halt, many suffering minor damage. Unfortunately, the

mines were not powerful enough to damage the hulls, but their occupants were severely shaken by the blasts, and many tracks were damaged.

All this time our anti-tank guns were engaging targets in spirited fashion … but gradually these light guns were knocked out, the crews suffering heavy casualties. By a miraculous turn of good fortune the tank attack had been halted when it seemed at Battalion Headquarters that they were likely to overrun 'B' Company and go on to attack the Blue Line behind us.

During the whole of the daylight hours … Captain Clapham had been directing fire from his regiment … undoubtedly this fire held up the tank attack by keeping the tanks closed down, and preventing clear visibility due to the clouds of dust. Even a direct hit, however, could not put a tank permanently out of action as the range was too long and the shells were high explosive, not armour-piercing.

The anti-tank guns of 24th and 26th Anti-Tank companies and 'J' Battery RHA were gradually forced out of action. Their crews had fought bravely with inadequate guns – largely captured Italian. The firefight went on all day … by early evening all at Battalion Headquarters were weary as they entered a second night under continuous fire and without sleep. Anxiety mounted as we realised that many of our forward posts were now in enemy hands, and we knew nothing certain of the fate of our men.

During the afternoon, Italian infantry without tanks failed against posts S8, S9 and S10, but Headquarters did not know, as signals had broken down. Brigadier Ray Tovell ordered the neighbouring battalion, the 2/23rd, to find out what had happened, or if necessary, control the posts. Captain Ian Malloch's company moved out at dusk, fired on by mortars and artillery, with anti-tank guns firing on the Bren gun carriers protecting their flanks.

Chester Wilmot described what they found: 'S10 was still held by Lieutenant J.S. Rosel and half a dozen men, although it was under heavy fire from positions beyond. These seven had beaten off several enemy attacks and had only a thousand rounds of ammunition left.' Malloch's men found S8 still held by five unwounded survivors with only a few hundred rounds left, then moved to fight off Italians who had surrounded Lt Christie's men in S9. They captured 33 men.

At daylight on 2 May, the battalion was relieved by the 2/10th Battalion.

It was years before anyone heard details of the fate of the overrun troops. Major Len Fell, on return from a POW camp, described how two German tanks bombarded Post S1 from a range of 100 to 200 yards:

> Eventually I saw Walker and his men being brought out of the pit … these tanks then moved to S2 and when within 200 yards they concentrated on the sangars and pits, blowing away the sandbags and destroying the sangars. Each tank had two or three infantry men riding on the tank ... under cover of the tank fire, [they] eventually dropped grenades into the weapon pit. We then surrendered and were taken out by the tank crews.

> When we came out of the pit we counted about forty German armoured vehicles. At this time there were no Italian infantry in sight and only a small number of Germans, mostly riding on tanks.
>
> The system of defence in the old Italian posts was unsuited to our weapons. We had no effective anti-tank weapon and the anti-tank pit was a death trap for LMG [light machine gun] and riflemen.

These posts were under clear observation of the Germans and Italians and it was only possible to improve sangars at night. Years later he expanded his report to the Official Historian (excerpts):

> The Germans had obviously learned a lesson from the Easter battle, as on this occasion they mopped up with tanks and Panzer Grenadiers before any infantry came in, in daylight.
>
> They used tanks to escort the prisoners to Acroma. Their behaviour was extremely correct, they cared for our wounded and allowed no looting by their own men or the Italians. They showed surprise that the Stuka attack had not frightened us out, and said that had invariably happened in the battles in Europe. I should like to emphasise how much German morale was helped by having planes over the battlefield all the time and by the example of Rommel, who was always well forward in the battle area. Several Germans said to me, 'Have you seen our General? He is right up here.'

Lieutenant Lachy Walker's 8 Platoon was among those overrun:

> At first light Neil Jones was killed and Aub Jarret wounded by one of the many tanks … 'Bugs' McLarty and Frank Simpson were both blown back into the pit while trying to mount an old Iti mortar gun. Others who tried to attack the tanks at first light were forced to take cover from the tank's 75 mm guns. All our Mills bombs and Iti grenades were expended and I, myself, with Sergeant Sam Fry, Pop Oram and Mont Montgomery were blown up in our gun emplacement through a tank shell explosion.
>
> Our only gratification after being winkled out of our pit, in our dumbfounded, incredulous and shocked condition, was to see the large number of dead 'Jerries' around the posts we were so keen to defend.

'C' Company suffered badly. Consider Post S4, under Corporal Rod Deering: 'Haphazard, spasmodic fighting went on all night, during which we wiped out a couple of groups of Ities with hand grenades. At first light on May 1 it was really on … we scrapped pretty solidly all morning with only one casualty, 'Tarzan' Kleinitz. A bullet went into his eye and came out the opposite side of his head … he was my No. 1 Bren gunner. About 11am Jerry brought up a couple of tanks … right up to point blank range and then let us have it. They blew the tops off the pits and we couldn't even stick up our heads to take a look, so I called the boys together and we discussed the situation. We decided the only thing we could do was to give it away, as we knew the posts on our right, half right, and half left had gone, and we were, more or less, entirely on our own. We were the last post to go.

When the Jerries came into the pit the officer, who spoke very good English, congratulated all of us and said we had put up an excellent fight.

Similar stories were told by others whose posts were overrun.

THE DIGGER WITH THE CORNET

As my father would never talk about combat, we are lucky to have an eyewitness from his platoon – Private Harry Frazer.

By our great good fortune, Harry Frazer was sent to my father's platoon on the eve of the Battle of the Salient. His intimate letters home speak for the common experience of the Rats of Tobruk. Here is a legend brought to life, a vivid, moving and sometimes brutally honest account of the average Digger enduring the terror and tedium that was the siege.

While John Rosel packed a camera to war, Harry carried a cornet.

Among Tobruk's treasures of human documents are some of the 181 letters Harry wrote to his parents Robert and Gwynnivere during Army service. His daughter Christina Westmore-Peyton donated them to the Australian War Memorial in 2002. They have never before been published.

Harry grew up at Swan Hill, where his Irish ancestors had settled in the 1850s.

Like rural kids of his era, he grew up rabbiting with a .22 rifle, and fishing in the Murray. He shared the family's absorption with music, playing cornet and trumpet in a local band. From St Mary's primary school and Swan Hill High School he joined the family business – hardware, and the regional funeral parlour.

While military authorities are sometimes derided for placing round pegs in square holes, at least here someone suspected anyone keen enough to master the three keys of a cornet might be invaluable in the 2/24th band – at least until fighting threatened.

In an era when soldiers rarely described the horrors of war so as not to distress families (or upset the officer censoring letters), Harry Frazer wrote frankly of the shock and confusion of combat, the threat of what we call Post Traumatic Stress Disorder, and the conflict between his deeply-held religious beliefs and what was seen over the sights of his Bren gun. He was soon to concede, as he wrote on May 19, 'I feel no longer, the urge for adventure, but have a great longing to get home and never leave again. The job has to be finished though, to make that possible.'

Where John Rosel had written his frontline message with urgency and military grace under pressure, with his intended recipients a hazardous journey away for a runner in peril, Harry's communications over 15,000 km took weeks to arrive. Written in reflection, they opened up significantly over the weeks. They were censored by my father, with no apparent excisions or redactions.

We pick up his letters immediately after the most intense period of the Battle of the Salient.

May 4, 1941

VX 41179 FRAZER DH

Dear Mother and Dad

I am writing this from the front line, where I have been for a week now, we moved up last Thursday night. Our band has been broken up, and we have all been places in different companys. At the moment I am attached to C Coy, with Ern Moffat. Things are pretty hot up here believe me, but I'm hoping for the best. We have been in action, some of it pretty fierce, and just at present are in rather a tight spot, but we are hoping for relief soon now. Sleep is a thing that one has to grab when he can now, as we are continuously on the lookout for the enemy who has been very active all this week, on top of it all Mother I'm homesick.

… I received at last Win's [his future wife] first parcel, the raisins were in good order and the socks and writing paper will be very useful. Try and not worry too much Mother, I'm looking after myself as much as is possible, and trusting in Our Lord to being me home safely to you all again.

… Tons of love to you both, as well as all my brothers and sisters

Always your loving son

Harry

PS Things are just anyhow here at the moment, and anything can happen. It will be rather a shock to you I suppose to learn that I am in action, but that's just the position and doing my best to look after myself, believe me.

May 10, 1941
C Coy 2/24
Dear Mother and Dad

I'm writing this now from behind the lines, we have come back a little way for a spell, and believe me it's well earned. … I think I can safely tell you now that we are at Tobruk and have been very nearly up to Benghazi. I'd love to see the papers just now, and what they have to say about things, over here now!

From what I have seen now, I feel very proud to be fighting with the AIF they are marvellous, with tons of guts. I have had a few narrow squeaks so far, have been right in the thick of it, and have seen quite enough for a while. The German is a very dirty fighter, and I feel no compunction now whatever to doing whatever little I can do towards wiping him out … after some of the things I have seen. I first went into action at approx. 8pm on April 30 and for 7 days after that it was hell let loose but thank God I came through alright. We were very lucky in our section only having two slight casualties out of the 10 of us, while between us we managed to give Jerry a pretty hot time.

It seems hard, doesn't it, to think that we have to fight so hard for this country when such a short time ago it was being glorified so brazenly in the papers as a smashing victory over the Dagoes. Of course, we are fighting the Germans now, their armoured divisions is what has been causing all the trouble, their infantry is not a patch on ours, although they are gamer than the Dagoes, but the general opinion now seems to be that he is getting finished here. The English artillery here are marvellous, I take my hat off to them. [On air combat.] Our boys are bringing them down every day, although he has been doing a lot of dive bombing, which is pretty awful.

May 19

… we had a very fierce day on Saturday. It's a big strain here and we are all hoping we will get relief soon as most of us have been fighting now for 6 weeks. I've had some very hard shocks lately (pals & mates etc) of which you will hear more anon …

… We are all heartily sick of this business and badly need a spell away out of it altogether. This is a war of nerves with shelling and dive bombing have seen a few bad cases of shell shock, and it's a wonder I haven't been myself at times its been that close. Have had two encounters at close quarters with Jerry, and his infantry is not a patch on ours, without his mechanised support. It's surprising how afraid one can be before an engagement, and then when he gets into it he seems to lose all fear, that's my experience anyway. But Oh Mother it's horrible this warfare, I've seen some horrible sights, and feel very sad at the moment, and want to forget it all, but am afraid it will be a day or two before we are out of this yet. We are constantly on guard here of course night and day …

May 24
I'm sitting in a dugout with Ern Moffat … and it's a filthy day just one continued duststorm here now [the khamsin]. In one way it's a blessing, as it makes visibility bad for the dive bombers, who are rather terrifying at times, although really do little damage … I can appreciate now, just what a hell it must be for the people in England …

I've seen with my own eye here, the dirty swine deliberately dive on a hospital marked with huge red crosses, and drop bombs right on it. It's good to see them come crashing down in flames. we had rather an exciting time a few days ago. We were moving up to a new position when Jerry spotted us … for about a quarter of an hour he dropped shells all around us, until we got below a hill, do you think I said a silent prayer when we got there, the closest one to me was about 10 yards off, which is quite close enough, thank you, if you could see me burrowing into the ground when one whistles, you'd reckon I'd make a first class rabbit. We see lots of funny little angles to this business, but only after the show is over, it's far from funny when it's on …

Gosh, I'd love a hot bath, some clean clothes and some green grass to lay on, or look at. It's over two months since I had a fresh water wash all over, I'll never moan about a Swan Hill duststorm again, when I get back, they are heaven to this country.

I can't understand why anybody should want to fight for this flare-up, although it is an ideal battleground, there is nothing to be destroyed just barren sand and stones.

... That medal which Sister Columbus sent me is appreciated, and I have placed it on the cord around my neck, together with some other medals and my identity discs.

... The other day we had some German prisoners coming through, and one of the boys got a pair of rosary beads off one of them, would you believe that, although the fact that the Jerry gave them to him makes me think they may have been propaganda. Somehow I can't bring myself to taking personal things off them, I know how I would feel if they did that to me. Most of them seem really glad to be taken prisoner and get out of it, and a lot of them speak perfect English, one chap ... was a chef in a London hotel before the war.

... will you tell Monica [his sister] that my platoon commander is John Rosel, whose sister is working with her in the Mercy [nurse Nancy Rosel, at the Mercy Hospital in Melbourne].

Harry injected some local colour:

May 29

... there's no such thing as a tree here, and very little of anything but sand and stone, about 14 million flies per man – it's lovely.

We don't get much news here, just little dibs and drabs, and it's jolly hard to form an idea of how things are going at all.

Mother, I'm brown as a berry, but I think half of it is dirt …

Four weeks later, he gave more details of the Battle of the Salient:

It's a very remarkable sight to see those German dive bombers in action. They come over at a terrific height, and dive straight down on the target at terrific speed, one wonders how they ever pull up … as a matter of fact, I've seen two of them dive straight into the ground and with their load of bombs you can imagine how much is left of them.

I think I can tell you now, that when our battalion first moved into the front, we went into the very position where the Jerries first tried to break through, so you can imagine things were fairly hectic for a while. A man learns a lot of things about himself in this game, and also about others too, and what surprises there are at times. How much a fellow takes for granted back home, a thousand little things which meant nothing to me at home mean such a lot now.

May 31

How the time is flying isn't it, here is nearly half 1941 gone, and it is 7 months since that Monday morning I set off from old Swannie, at times it seems like 7 years.

We thought we were going to do an attack last night, everybody was standing to in full battle order, just waiting for the word to go in, but about 9.30 word came through it was off – we all heaved a sigh of relief and relaxed. A man thinks of a thousand things, when he is waiting to go a stunt like that, wondering whether he going to be lucky or otherwise, and it's then that he thinks of all the things at home which mean to much to him. You realise Mother, don't you, that I am taking a very active part in this business now, band work is a thing of the past,

… I have settled down into my new job, as a rifleman, I got a pretty bad initiation didn't I, but still, am feeling a lot more satisfied than I was before they broke us up.

Somehow it made me feel very guilty, when we were together as a band, to be skulking away back in comparative safety, when the rest of the boys in the battalion were out in front, with the chance of going into action any day.

This war is a rotten business and has taken some bonza chaps, that I know, and you know. But I must try and keep off that line.

… I am glad to have the opportunity to hear Mass tomorrow, for the first time for 6 weeks … the best I have been able to do is read my Missal each Sunday, and believe me, I've read it in some queer places. … one Sunday perched behind a machine gun, ready to pour lead into the first Hun who showed his head, which really is not a very edifying mixture, but duty is duty, is it not, and I feel now, after some of the things I've seen and heard, about the German, by that I mean the leaders, not the poor unfortunate private soldier who doesn't want the war any more than we do, and is only acting under orders, I feel that we are fighting for our freedom and self-respect.

I am very proud to belong to this AIF and to have taken part in the action I did – it was really a great experience, and I was very lucky, here's hoping, God will look after me still further.

… the meals haven't been too bad but water is rationed, and is a bit salty to drink, one dreams of long cool beers and icy cold tomato sandwiches, oh boy, how would they go down right now – I'd be drunk for a week.

... I know it will be a terrible shock to many to hear about Tommy Wilkins. I was only about 200 yards away from where he got hit, in a pillbox we were holding. There was a terrific artillery barrage coming over, falling all round us, and very fierce fighting going on. You can assure his friends if it will help at all, that I saw what happened, and it was quite instantaneous, he never knew what hit him, a shell must have landed right at his feet. You can imagine the shock I got … but you've just got to try and ride out these things here, one could easily go to pieces at some of the things he sees.

The desert climate:

The heat is very dry and clear, very similar to the clear heat in Swan Hill, the difference being that there is absolutely no shade whatever, only what you make yourself in the dugout, and its like an oven in there to say nothing of the flies. The nights here are glorious though, delightfully cool and bright, and easily the most beautiful nights I've ever seen, just made for walking out, or parking on a nice green lawn … then from about 3 onwards it gets quite chilly and blankets are necessary.

June 23

BHQ [Battalion Headquarters]

At long last the mail arrived after a spell of more than a month without any. Well, Mother, for a start I must tell you that it was somewhat of a surprise to me, to learn I had been posted missing. I know that quite a few of us in our particular platoon had been reported missing at Battalion HQ, but I had been assured that we turned up in time to prevent any need to inform you at home.

I think I can now tell you what actually happened, you must have had a very worrying week, before the other cable arrived telling you I was safe.

To start with we first went into action on April 30, when Jerry attacked, right at the point where our Bn was holding. He opened his attack in the afternoon with dive bombing, and machine gunning from the air, on our positions (which incidentally is the most terrifying experience I have ever known, and want to know). Although he went very close at times, he did not do any serious damage. He then opened up, about 7.30pm, with a terrific artillery barrage which he kept up for two hours solid, whilst his tanks and infantry moved up to within 2,000 yards of us. The shelling was terrific, and I don't know to this day how one shell in particular missed me, it was very close. He then moved in to attack us with tanks and very heavily equipped infantry. After that I have not a very clear recollection of what really happened. There were huge tanks everywhere, and swarms of Dagoes and Jerrys, the noise was terrific and bullets and shrapnel were flying everywhere. There were 8 of us holding our little link in the chain, and we luckily managed to make it a bit too hot for the blighters who came at us. At one time, there were over 200, attacking out little fortress, and I honestly have very little recollection of what actually took place. All I know is, we stood there and blazed away until at last the enemy retired. Not one of the eight of us were hit, and between us we had stopped easily a hundred of the Jerries, their stretcher bearers were working like blazes all that night and half the following day. Well then when things finally quietened down, and we had a look around, we found we were isolated with the enemy in possession of positions not 3,000 yards behind us and to our left.

It looked like a spell in Jerryland for us for a while, as we were nearly out of ammo, had no water and only a few tins of bully and some biscuits. If he had attacked us then he could have taken our little force easily, but he had, as I learned later suffered terrific casualties gaining what little ground he did, and was probably licking his wounds. It gave us a spell, although we had had no sleep for two nights and were absolutely done in.

Then we got the thing we least expected. Another battalion, had heard of our position, and had sent along 16 men to help us. You can imagine how glad we were to see them. That night our boys (AIF) counter-attacked, and took back some of the posts we had lost, and we were able to get food, water and ammo. We were still lost as far as our own unit was concerned, and attached ourselves to the people who had come to our assistance. For two days we were in this position, and at last were apparently located and relieved, or at least went back a little way and rejoined what was left of the poor old 24th. The odds against us in the attack were terrific, and I consider honestly that our boys did a wonderful job to hold the Germans, against heavy and light tanks, flame throwers, dive bombing and machine gunning. I have learned since, from a captured Prussian officer, that it was the most fierce action since the Battle of the Somme. Now that it is over (for the present) I feel very proud to have been one of the few, who have actually held, for the first time in this war, a determined and carefully planned German attack. We have heard since from information from P.O.W.s that they were determined to take the position at all costs, and got a very unpleasant surprise when they failed. I have been in several smaller actions since, and am truly grateful to the 'One' who I am sure is responsible for bringing me through. That

> I think Mother will help to explain how it was I was posted missing for a few days.
>
> It is a very great experience for anyone who comes through, and I have altered and broadened a lot of my ideas lately.

He was posted from frontline duties to the Battalion Headquarters:

> I have told you in a previous letter that I have got a new job, as a clerk at Bn HQ, and each day becoming more used to the routine, and gradually settling into it. It is a job which carries a fair amount of responsibility and one which I am hoping will tighten up a lot of slackness which I know is present in my makeup. That is the chief reason why I took it on. Army discipline demands, the most care and exactness in the keeping of records of various items, of which quite a few are my job to look after, and any mistakes are mine, and am held responsible for same.
>
> … it is just like a business, exactly the same, records, invoices, receipts, filing etc, and errors are not permitted. Life in general here has become very dull, absolutely no variety at all, and we have been here now since March, nearly 4 months … I haven't seen a white woman for 4 months nor a female of any description for 4. Pictures and bright lights are memories, and a real pot of beer is something one dreams about.
>
> My cornet is safely packed away in a truck chest

here at B.H.Q. I am thinking seriously of sending it home if it is not too heavy.

… Have just heard news that Germany is marching on Russia, my word, that is taking on some job, I'll say. I think he might be biting off more than he can chew …

* * *

The May Show was a disaster for the 2/24th Battalion, whose history notes:

> few AIF battalions had a more severe introduction to battle … in our first major action we lost three rifle company commanders and more than six rifle platoons of the 12 in the battalion.

The award of John Rosel's Military Cross appeared in the *London Gazette* of 19 August 1941. The citation:

> At Tobruk, Lieut John Rosel was in command of a platoon occupying three posts when enemy attacked on evening of 30 April 1941. He displayed calmness and outstanding leadership when communications between his company H.Q. and B.H.Q. had been severed by enemy artillery. His platoon fought off repeated attacks and held all three posts. After the enemy had captured his company headquarters he took control of the company, displayed initiative in making contact with B.H.Q. and with the unit on the right flank. He made several endeavours to relieve the company H.Q. and continued to hold posts against determined attacks.

Private Harry Frazer, c.1940.
From a family album.

'A sangar'
Tedium at Tobruk: One digger reads, another rests in a sangar (rock breastwork) in 14 platoon's defensive positions. Their Bren gun and tripod lie between them.

AFTER BATTLE

THE SIEGE CONTINUES

From 3 May the siege experience was routine for five months, with only brief flare-ups of fighting.

In outline:

> Intermittent artillery fire in the early mornings and late afternoons when the air was still and visibility relatively good; strong sunshine and dust storms during the day when the heat increased and the breeze rose; vehicles moving along the tracks six inches deep in fine dust causing intermittent palls of white and yellow powder to rise and sweep along behind the movement … the standard dress by day was a pair of ragged khaki shorts, socks around the ankles, boots turning white with scuffling on the sand and rocks and a battered sand-coloured tin hat or khaki fur-felt [slouch hat]. As the siege went on men lost weight and fined down, but most found

> the climate congenial and healthy in spite of occasional attacks of dysentery and the ever-present desert sores which were hard to heal once the skin was grazed.
>
> Dig, dig and dig again were the orders as the infantry struggled to improve their posts.

Night patrolling developed to keep the enemy in a constant state of tension.

On 15 May the so-called Composite Company formed after the losses of the May Show was renamed 'A' Company, with Lt Rosel one of its platoon commanders.

Fighting resumed on 16 May. John Rosel's platoon was used to reinforce two posts, but was not required for any other active role, although it was heavily shelled in the wadi it occupied.

An extract from Joe Maloney's later report:

> Orders were given to move forward to [Post] S13 on the perimeter and the Pl led by Lt Rosel carrying ammunition boxes left the shelter of the wadi and moved across the flat in open formation. During this advance they were under enemy observation and were subjected to shell fire which caused two casualties (Privates Winch and Anthony being wounded by shrapnel).
>
> Advancing 2,000 yards across open country, their pace limited to a steady walk by the ammunition boxes they were carrying, the platoon reached the comparative shelter of a small wadi 1,000 yards rear of the Red Line. Whilst here two enemy planes flew very low overhead but left them unmolested. To cover the last 1,000 yards

> the platoon was sent forward in groups of three men and were subjected to machine gun fire throughout the journey. Reaching S12 they rested while a party of German POWs marched out past them. Here Corporal Crawley's section … had to traverse a wadi under direct observation … although under mortar fire they succeeded in reaching their objective safely with all gear and ammunition intact.

The battalion was relieved on 24 May and spent four days cleaning up a rear post, siting new and improving existing works. They welcomed their first issue of a dozen Thompson submachine guns – 'Tommy guns'.

The battalion was being returned to full strength as destroyers brought in soldiers and supplies on a hazardous night run from Egypt, with less than an hour available around midnight to unload reinforcements, ammunition, ordnance spares and food, and embarkation of 'useless mouths'. Around 22,000 troops remained by the end of May.

Colonel Spowers imbued the battalion with his own spirit of enthusiasm for the task ahead, facing months of physical discomfort, hard living and boredom. He was developing the 'essential resiliency of spirit necessary in an infantry battalion, which was destined to carry on efficiently after giving and receiving many hard knocks through nearly five more years of arduous warfare,' the history says.

On June 11 the battalion was back in the front line.

> Across most of our front ran an anti-tank ditch excavated by the Italians after immense labour … wire ran right

> across the front and around the concrete posts. Mines and booby traps abounded, and great care was needed in taking the correct paths through the minefields – no easy task for a tired patrol returning after being out most of the night.

There was some dodgy work with mines, especially the feared 'jumping jack' anti-personnel mine. The sappers became familiar with the German Teller mines and in a supreme example of scrounging, dug some up for recycling into Australian minefields.

Harry Frazer gave his parents a vivid picture of life in the Salient once the fighting had died down.

> *14 October*
>
> The day here is the worst we have ever had up this way, there is a very strong West wind blowing and bringing with all the dust in Libya. I have never seen anything like it even in Swanee and believe me a duststorm here has got anything the mallee can produce licked hollow. The day does not go black the way it does up there, but the effect is far worse believe me. Imagine a steady stream of fine sand bowling along at a fair rate, at most times impossible to see beyond 8 to 10 feet, and continuing unabatingly for anything up to 12 hours, burying anything laying on the ground, and filling every crack and hole, dugouts included with a layer of sand sometime a foot deep.
>
> Meals are a problem as you may well imagine, they are eaten in the open here at all times, and dinner today

was awful. Bloke will have a fair lining on his stomach when he leaves this place, and should be able to tackle anything at all in the way of food, the only thing we haven't had a crack at is grass and the reason for that is simply there is none here. But all jokes aside, the cook is doing a marvellous job, considering the conditions under which he has to work, and material he has to work with. I know you will be interested to know a little of what we get to eat here Mother, so will give you a detailed description of last nights tea, which meal by the way is the most popular one here. We are very fortunate in having a cook who takes a pride in making the evening meal as attractive as he can, and he does a remarkably good job.

Last night he put on a potato pie flavoured with onions which was very palatable and in plenty: to follow he had made up a dish of custard plentifully reinforced with tinned Pineapple and Peach, cooked in a large dish and divided into squares, each square being topped off with about two table-spoons of chocolate sauce, it was delightful and the cause of many doubling back for a second helping, yours truly well in the forward posn ... tonight's tea was just as good and appetising, in fact for the last three weeks we haven't had a crook meal in the evening. Nobody eats much for dinner, a cup of tea and a slice of bread and jam seems to satisfy me, and for breakfast there is porridge and the eternal bacon. Whatever you do Mother, when I come home, don't give me bacon, I think I have had eaten enough of the stuff to do me for the next 50 years.

He changes mood:

> Life here on the whole is not so bad … the only thing is the monotony of the old flat desert, nothing to do at night, with complete blackness wherever you go, which is usually from one dugout to another, I am forgetting though we do have some entertainment here, and that is when Jerry comes over at night to lay a few eggs around. I have seen some unforgettable sights when our Ack Ack opens up, and searchlights come on. The display of fireworks has got Henley licked to a frazzle. Tracers of all colours shooting up in all directions, the flash of the heavy guns and the searchlights darting about the sky make a wonderful sight … occasionally a plane is hit and then we see a rather awesome sight of a blazing meteor falling through the sky. But I'm beginning to get morbid …
>
> I have heard that since we have been here there has been in round figures, 2,500 air raids … the amazing thing is the small amount of damage done. I have my cornet, and at night often have a bit of a blow, a few of the boys come round and we have a song or two, and sometimes a chap who has a piano accordion comes over and we have a real treat.

There were often touches of humour:

> We have an issue of cigarettes from the English Comfort Fund each week (50 cigarettes) but they are very ordinary

> … in between we have to make do with Italian Army issue cigarettes which in my opinion are foul, in fact, I'd rather smoke horse manure!

* * *

The reinforcement depot in Palestine was now properly established and in need of battle-experienced officers and NCOs. John Rosel had had good health, apart from a painful episode of prepatellar bursitis, an inflammation of the bursa (a fluid-filled sac at the front of the knee) which hospitalised him for 17 days in August 1941. On 20 August Lieutenants Rosel and Macfarlane were among those seconded to 26 Australian Infantry Training Battalion in Palestine (John was appointed company Commander) in theory for a six-month period: they never returned to Tobruk.

About this time, my father made a commitment to the future. Lorna and John had a long-distance engagement, announced in *The Herald* (Melbourne), on 29 September 1941. His (deliberately?) blurred photo from Tel Aviv was captioned 'Lorna's ring before it left Palestine. Bit bashful'. It was possibly at the same time he bought an intricately-woven wire circular brooch, one of few souvenirs we know of.

He was promoted temporary captain on 28 October, relinquishing this rank on his return to regimental duties on 23 December. He was selected for duty in Australia on 7 February 1942 and embarked on the *Dorset* on 23 March. He disembarked at the 4th Military District, South Australia, and then served briefly at the 3rd Military District Training Depot at Fitzroy, Melbourne.

* * *

In Tobruk, the supply position improved, with limited cigarettes and sweets available for purchase.

The advance party of the battalion left Tobruk by sea on October 18 on an Australian destroyer, with the remainder sailing two days later on the minelayer *Latona* and the destroyer HMAS *Nizam*.

There was a numbing conclusion to their desert service. A large wave washed 20 of them overboard from *Nizam*'s deck. Against the Navy's standing orders, *Nizam* stopped to rescue men swimming fully-clothed and without lifebelts. Six men were lost, believed drowned, while another six were reported accidentally injured at sea. Corporal Denis Horan died later from injuries received.

'The battalion looked a scarecrow lot on reaching Alexandria,' the history notes. 'In their stained and greasy tunics and trousers, boots that had not seen polish for months and sand-coloured tin hats, they were far from a natty-looking outfit.'

> All old Tobruk hands always look back on the place with some kind of affection. Perhaps this is because life there was stripped down to fundamental elements and because each man of each arm and service knew that his job was essential and must be carried out properly because of the interdependence of all, one on another. We also found out what material elements were essential for survival in the face of the enemy. Techniques of defensive warfare were developed which proved invaluable at Alamein and, perhaps most important of all, each battalion realised that it was not fighting its own private war.
>
> Confidence was developed within the battalion … in later years, when it became possible to review the siege

in better perspective, it was realised that the garrison had carried out a feat of endurance worthy to rank with some of the greatest epics of history.

So far as the men of the battalion were concerned, they felt at the end of the siege that they had carried through what they had been called on to do. They were weary, they wanted some relief from the inevitable round of daily duty, and they wanted to participate again in some more normal form of living. They were, however, quietly confident of their own ability to cope with any task to be handed out in the future.

Peter Atkinson contributed poetry to the battalion's *Furphy Flyer* roneoed newssheet. An excerpt:

The Salient

No artist's scene and there is no green
Nor grass, nor shade, nor water.
No birds to fly and sing in the sky,
Just the crash of the shell and mortar.
Just flat, drab sand – upsweeping land
And stunted camel thorn.
Just the outline sharp of the stony scarp
Of the wadis deep and worn,
No structures tall to relieve it all
Lest we give position away,
Just the barbed wire tie etched against the sky
And the nets of the arty bay.
['Arty' was an abbreviation for artillery.]

Tobruk: The Battalion Toll

Killed In Action or died of wounds: 5 officers and 67 other ranks;

Died from other causes: 17 other ranks;

Wounded: 9 officers and 83 other ranks;

Prisoners of war: 255.

Overall, the Australians had 3,009 casualties at Tobruk: 832 killed, 941 prisoners of war.

A padre (right) concludes the burial service as a Digger's body is lowered and his comrades fire a volley over his grave. Captioned in Harry Frazer's family album only as 'Burial Middle East.'
Harry was familiar with death: his family were funeral directors at Swan Hill.

Camp Julis, Palestine

26 October 1941–12 January 1942

The highlight of the return to Palestine was the accumulated mail.

> Julis Camp was a permanent camp with suitable amenities, including wet and dry canteens, a cinema, YMCA hut and showers – unimaginable luxury indeed after Tobruk. Orange groves were a relief to eyes which had endured desert glare and windblown sand. Training was limited to five hours a day, food was supplemented by the arrival of previously undelivered food parcels from Australia and the tents were littered with food and books – Aussie beer was in more than ample supply.

Syria

13 January–24 June 1942

The battalion moved to Syria for garrison duty, based about six miles east of Tripoli. They guarded vast ammunition dumps, and with officers going off to various schools, the battalion resembled a tourist centre enquiry office.

A platoon camped on the sea front near Tripoli to watch for possible German landing parties dined well on fresh fish, until the lieutenant discovered that the number of grenades was shrinking.

All was peaceful training until they heard that Rommel had attacked the Gazala line in strength, forcing the Eighth Army back to the frontier. On 21 June Tobruk was overcome with huge losses of men and material.

(During this time Lt Rosel and Captain Gus Oakley were selected to return to Australia. They did not rejoin the battalion until 1944.)

Tel El Eisa and El Alamein

The battalion returned to the Western Desert and fought at Tel El Eisa (July) and in the great battle of El Alamein (October–November) which was to be regarded as one of the turning points of the war.

Winston Churchill was later to say of the battle of El Alamein: 'Now this is not the end. It is not even the beginning of the end, but it is, perhaps, the end of the beginning.'

It was certainly the end for the battalion's 119 dead at El Alamein.

Harry was to tell his family that a mate went to help a wounded soldier, and was shot dead. Harry went out himself and was shot in the left arm. 'All of my mates were dead,' he would say postwar in a rare comment. 'I don't know how I got through the six years.'

Among the dead were soldiers from John Rosel's photographs, including 'Gee Gee' Anderson and Terry Jones.

Regimental Sergeant Major Jim Nicoll spoke of 20 trucks waiting to take the battalion after handing over to another battalion. The transport officer was angry at the delay, fearing being caught there by daylight: 'I wish they would bloody well hurry up.' Nicoll told him 'We *are* here', only to be asked 'When are the rest of your mob going to get here'. He replied: 'Well, Sir, if that is your big worry, you can leave three or four trucks and amble the rest of them off. We won't require any more … this is the 2/24th Australian Infantry Battalion.'

'He peered closely into my face and when he saw I was not being funny, he just said "God Almighty!" and went on his way.'

Then there were the casualties of the mind. The Regimental

Medical Officer had a system for avoiding the evacuation of those suffering 'neurosis' – or shell shock. They were bedded down in slit trenches around the regimental aid post and given massive doses of the barbiturate sedative phenobarbital. 'A day's sleep, and several good feeds, and the "casualty" was usually fit, well and ready to return to duty', the history concludes. (It would be decades before returned soldiers were offered treatment for post-traumatic stress disorder.)

The battalion's last patrol against the enemy in the Western Desert was on 3 November 1942. It left Alamein in the first week of December and sailed for Australia on 1 February 1943, reaching Melbourne on 25 February.

'Batman: Terry Jones'
Lt Rosel's platoon, 'C' Company, Tobruk, July 1941.
A *batman* or an orderly is a soldier assigned to a commissioned officer as a personal servant. A year later, Terry Jones was among 119 soldiers of the battalion killed at El Alamein.

AUSTRALIA AND THE PACIFIC

When John returned to Melbourne, photographs of his reunion with Lorna featured in two Melbourne papers on 5 May 1942. They married at Xavier College chapel a week later.

He was seconded to 34 Australian Infantry Training Battalion on 21 May 1942, and appointed second in-command 2 Infantry Special Group on 28 May 1943. He was appointed captain on 24 December 1943.

Without him, the battalion worked hard at the jungle training area on the Atherton Tablelands, Queensland, between 8 April and 31 July 1943.

It moved to New Guinea and fought at Lae, Finschhafen, Sattelberg, and Wareo, ending its fighting role in New Guinea on 22 December and returning to Australia on 1 March 1944.

Harry Frazer's great cobber, Ern Moffatt, was killed by a sniper during the Lae battle: 'Yes, Dad, it was a great shock when Ernie was killed,' he wrote. 'I felt as if I had lost a brother.' He was later to say, 'I feel very much on my own now, with so many of the old original boys gone.'

John received his MC at the Governor-General's Investiture at Admiralty House, Sydney, on 23 June 1944. By Christmas 1944, only four of the original officers of the battalion remained – Captains Serle, Rosel, Ebell and Macfarlane. After further training at Ravenshoe on the Atherton Tablelands, the battalion sailed to Morotai, en route to fight at Tarakan in Borneo just before the war ended – a campaign sometimes assessed as unnecessary.

John Rosel rejoined the battalion and served at Tarakan in the Left Out of Battle group, comprising officers and men kept behind to provide reinforcements to key roles and help reconstitute the battalion after combat. Unlike his comrade Harry Frazer, he dodged malaria, which was to recur to plague Harry for life.

A final irony. Notwithstanding the best efforts of Germans, Italians, Japanese and inhospitable combat zones, he survived to the end of the war, if in considerable discomfort: 21 days after the battalion celebrated the Japanese surrender, Captain Rosel was evacuated sick to Australia, suffering from haemorrhoids (piles). To paraphrase the poet T.S. Eliot, his world of war ended 'not with a bang but a whimper' … but a pain in the arse.

PEACE?

John Rosel served in the AIF outside Australia for 757 days, and within Australia for 1,098 days. Demobilised on 13 December 1945, he resumed at the bank in February 1946. He returned to a teller's post, often with a loaded .38 pistol within sight (no Occupational Health and Safety concerns) to deter anybody emulating the Kelly Gang, which held up National Banks at Euroa and Jerilderie in the late 1870s. I hate to think what might have happened if someone threatened his staff.

Like any prudent bank teller, he had saved most of his wartime pay, a healthy 1,905 pounds which was to contribute to buying an old weatherboard house at 61 Burwood Rd, Burwood, for a family grown to six kids by 1954. He may not have sired a platoon, but almost a section.

Burwood was on the edge of the postwar population explosion – we could get up to mischief in Stocksy's Paddocks and other undeveloped land, quickly to become suburbia. Burwood was a test case for Victoria's first supermarket and drive-in cinema. 'Progress' meant that the Country Roads Board compulsorily acquired our house to help create the Burwood Highway.

The family was necessarily frugal. Dad repaired our shoes, we kids were encouraged to help grow vegetables and we bottled fruit, and there was a once-only attempt to air-dry sliced beans on his waterproof Army poncho.

Lorna and John's childrearing practices included carryovers from the Good Officer school of caring for troops. 'Always dry between your toes … look after your feet and they will look after you' – perhaps he had memories of soft city-dwellers falling out of Bonegilla route marches with ailing feet. Our school shoes had to be polished, and even our Dunlop Volley OC canvas-upper tennis shoes had to be whitened: 'If you can't be a good tennis player, at least look like one!' Such humble military mantras were supported by a formidable demonstration of good example. Warm and empathetic, he was a man of total loyalties, generosity, and a big grin. We hated to let our hero down.

Although he was descended from at least three generations of innkeepers and hotel owners, he didn't drink beer, only the odd sherry with family celebrations, or once-removed in Grandma's famous sherry trifle. Gambling was reserved for the Melbourne Cup office sweep.

While his German ancestors were Lutheran, and often Masons, his indomitable mother raised her four children as Catholics in that more religious era when one in five Australians was Catholic.

With his smokes, pipe and inevitable hat lending a touch of gravitas, he was the picture of your friendly bank officer. We were not surprised by his promotion to manager, at the new Burwood branch, no less. Family lore has it that his first act was to boost his ledgers by transferring at least nine accounts – parents, six kids and Grandma – to Burwood.

But we discovered a flaw. To our disappointment he gently deflected any question about exactly how he won the Military Cross kept in his chest of drawers. This resulted in some of us developing a wide interest in military history to help understand the pressures on those who volunteer for war.

The only military relic visible in the house – probably because it was useful – was a large gaudy ashtray nicked from Shepheard's Hotel, a legendary Cairo institution which was 'Officers Only' for the duration. It resided on the mantlepiece above the fireplace, handy when card schools were convened by the adults.

Looking further, we dared to search the chest of drawers. What military wonders! First off, the medals, then a zipped officer's canvas map case, still displaying Tobruk's defences, with his chinagraph markings on the plastic overlay. There were old khaki clothes reserved for gardening, his officer's hat and tin helmet, a 45-mm Italian Brixia mortar bomb (minus explosive), a Sam Browne belt and sundry haversacks, … and deep down, an oiled cloth protecting his revolver, and bullets.

After many years, we dared to borrow it, going into the bush and failing to hit the lid of a 44-gallon drum at 10 paces. We sneaked it back (probably without cleaning it) and it was never seen again. Perhaps a lingering whiff of cordite persuaded him to get it away from the kids, while avoiding mutually embarrassing questions about what happened.

He didn't keep close to the battalion association, taking us to a couple of battalion picnic reunions early on, but to my recollection, did not attend Anzac Day commemorations, or join in Returned Services League (RSL) celebrations.

Apart from the cigarettes, not yet truly condemned as a health risk, he had one weakness, the Melbourne Football Club. The

Demons magically won five premierships in the glorious 50s, and went on to snatch the '64 flag before entering the wilderness. Joining dad at the football after the banks closed (yes, Saturday banking) was rather character building. He had to be a useful carpenter to expand the house and build cupboards for the horde, so it was easy to craft a folding footstool for No. 1 son to stand to see the footy better. He restrained himself barracking, apologising for a rare 'bloody hell' when the umpire let us down or someone whacked Ron Barassi, another hero.

One had to barrack warily, standing in the Outers of that great arc of suburban grounds, now mostly history or parks. In military terms, one did not stick one's head over the parapet at Collingwood's headquarters, Victoria Park. Best also to be modest in victory with schoolmates.

The last time I cried in public was the '58 grand final, lost to a combative Collingwood which ended our hope of four successive Grand Finals. As a 50-year member of the Melbourne Cricket Club, I hope I am around to cry again when we win our next Grand Final.

The camera rarely emerged to record the growing family. There are only a handful of images from Burwood and later. But he happily handed it over for me to take my first photos in the last week at high school. It's gone now, like almost all those military mementos. But I did wear his officer's cap in school cadets, where we fired the weapons he had used: rifle, Bren, and Owen gun. With his passion for order, he'd give a quick inspection of our uniform, to make sure we had wielded Blanco on belt and gaiters, and Brasso on buttons, to his satisfaction. A tough inspection. He was content with our modest exposure to military life – there were no cautionary tales or bitter remarks about conflict past.

Stray recollections would emerge: he might recall the impossibility of keeping a sharp edge on his razor in the desert. My brother Gerry quizzed him about a collection of gaudy Egyptian banknotes, and a few foreign coins. 'Not worth a brass razoo', he laughed in a fine example of old Australian slang, the razoo being a non-existent coin of no value. He added that troops going on leave would be given razoos (or other tokens, presumably) to avoid being robbed. The next morning the ladies of the foreign night, or their pimps, would come to the camp to exchange tokens for cash. That was his story, anyway.

I have a recollection that he still had some Italian grenade fragments in his neck.

Thirty years after the war, he opened up a little to his American son-in-law, Pat Parks, a Vietnam veteran: 'He told me a story about a bomber that flew over every night and dropped a few bombs. John said they would let the boys pop off a few shots at it with a captured Italian field piece of some sort. More for morale than effectiveness! We spoke of other war incidents that we could both relate to, that time has erased from my mind … I had a million more questions but sadly he passed before we could resume our conversation.' My sister Marita said that was the first time she had ever heard her dad speak of the war.

He was happy enough to indulge my growing interest in things military, giving me a copy of *The Cruel Sea,* Nicholas Monsarrat's grim tale of the Battle of the Atlantic. Aged around nine, I thought this was pretty liberal. Until I found out that the Cadet Edition meant the raunchy bits had been cut. (It was almost 70 years before I discovered he had been an official censor of his platoon's letters).

His Fair Go tradition carried into peacetime, if only to keep order among parents, six kids and Grandma. Sometime Fair Go had a life lesson too. When you were old enough to divvy up Mum's immortal lemon pudding, or the Christmas fruitcake, the Rosel with the knife always had last slice. Geometry education, anyone? At least as the oldest boy I was guaranteed new clothes.

Then tragedy struck again. Our warm family life collapsed when Lorna died of cancer at only 44 in September 1964. She had just helped celebrate my 21st birthday; I was the oldest.

By good fortune, dad married a friend of mum's since the 1930s, long known to us as honorary 'Aunty Marg' Butler, a single professional woman who nobly gave up her independence to help rear the tribe.

When financial pressures eased, Margaret and John were able to take some overseas trips, and dad even had the odd Scotch. Golf became possible. In 1973, with the youngest children, twins Tony and Patricia almost adults, and financial pressures easing, he retired from the bank for the calmer life of an office manager with friends at a suburban law firm. We lost a brother, Peter, to a heart condition which today would have been corrected.

Dad even risked the odd lottery ticket. We were stunned in 1980 to hear a rumour from a sibling that they had won one of the first huge Tattslotto prizes. Partly correct: they were in a syndicate of 14, and 13 syndicates had got up … instead of a spectacular retirement, he got a new set of golf clubs.

This rewarding second life ended with his death from lung cancer in 1981, aged only 64. General Rommel hadn't been able to stop him, but the bloody ciggies did, 40 years after those hours of mayhem at Post S10 at Tobruk. He died hard, tough to the last, but we expected nothing else – at least we were granted time to share our memories.

There was something of a poignant footnote to his decades of love and service when I ran across 'Uncle Ray' Walker – another Tobruk colleague and fellow Melbourne football club fanatic – at the Melbourne Cricket Ground in the 1990s. As the Demons went down in flames, again, this faithful supporter grumbled: 'Your old man would be turning in his grave at this performance'. He added, wistfully: 'I've never forgiven myself for swapping my ciggie ration for his beer ration at Tobruk.' Surely a quintessential Melbourne salute.

'MC Winner Home From Tobruk – Lt J.S. Rosel, who won the Military Cross at Tobruk, photographed today with his fiancée, Miss Lorna Knowles.' From the *Herald*, Melbourne, 5 May 1942.

Rye beach, Victoria, 1938.
Lorna Knowles (top left) my future mother, and her friend Margaret Butler (bottom left).
After Lorna died of cancer at 44, leaving six children, Margaret gave up her independent life to marry my father and help raise the children. Both brave, kind and strong women.

AFTERMATH

The Diggers – those not forever in Libya, where headstones in the Benghazi war cemetery were desecrated by an Islamist militia in 2012, and later restored – returned to their tractors, sheep and other rural pursuits, while city mates donned their 'demob' (demobilisation) suits and claimed back jobs in offices, schools and other civilian combat zones.

The battalion was disbanded in 1946. Postwar, the battalion association offered welfare support and arranged for members to visit the sick and ailing. It was granted Freedom of the City of Wangaratta in 1990 and it is a tradition for some members and their families to visit Wangaratta on the weekend after Melbourne Cup Day for a service at the cemetery, followed by a reunion dinner. In 2019 only one Digger – Hautrie Crick, 101 – was able to join the commemoration.

In 1997 the battalion erected at Wangaratta a memorial wall listing the names of 347 men killed in action or died of wounds. The battalion donates towards citizenship awards at the three Wangaratta high schools.

I interviewed **Alan Macfarlane** (quoted on pages 28–29) in 2013, when the old warrior was 94, although with excellent recall. There was a touching welcome, literally. He held his hand over my retreating hairline to check my facial likeness to dad. He was reflective as he gently turned the album's pages: So-and-so was killed. He disliked the CO who had turned down a recommendation for a medal for Alan. He still had nightmares, not about combat, more on the people.

Soldiers firing on either side of him were killed in one action, he recalled (2 May 1941). He regretted that dad had few postwar links with the battalion other than several early battalion picnics, taking one of the old Yarra ferries to the Hawthorn Tea Gardens, where Leonda Restaurant now stands. He concluded: 'The Military Cross? Your father earned it, I assure you.'

Harry Frazer had married Winifrid Esler while on leave in 1943. Later a sergeant, he served through the war and received a Commander-In-Chief's Commendation Card.

Harry and Winifrid adopted Christina and Michael and he left the family business to settle on a mixed farm outside Benalla in 1958. He remained active in the Returned Services League (RSL) and the Rats of Tobruk organisation, with its vital welfare component for returned men needing help, and Legacy, which has looked after the families of deceased servicemen and women since 1923. His music continued, including piano, and playing the organ at St Joseph's church. 'He was a fine dad,' Christina says. 'We were never aware of any war-related stresses. And while the bullet wound never bothered him, the Army had pulled out his teeth on enlistment, and he was always trying new dentures to suit his trumpet playing … when he died in 1994 I found a hundred pairs.'

In 1984 Harry personally donated the cornet which had once sounded over a desert battlefield to the Defence Force School of Music at Simpson Barracks, Watsonia, Victoria. Today it is displayed in their museum. By appointment, (03) 8481 7318.

While its brass may tarnish, the reputation of those it saluted never will.

Tobruk is not easily visited. In 2009 Christina made an emotional pilgrimage to the key Western Desert battlefields accompanied only by a driver and guide. This included a week in Tobruk. 'The old defence posts are still a wilderness,' she says. 'Debris everywhere, wire, rusting tins, bits of shell and bullets, any number of concrete trenches and firing posts.' She cried for days. 'So sad … I'm sorry I didn't ask dad more about the battle.'

A highlight was a visit to the famous Fig Tree underground Regimental Aid Post. The fig tree has seen some high-ranking Australians under its branches, commemorating the Diggers treated in the caves below. A cutting grows outside the Shrine of Remembrance in Melbourne, a living memorial. At Wangaratta, cuttings grow at the 2/24th Memorial Precinct at the cemetery, the RSL and the High School.

At El Alamein visitors are more cautious, with some mined areas off limits.

Harry's letters were the basis for Christina's thesis, *Spirituality on the Battlefield*.

The spartan huts at **Bonegilla** in northeast Victoria which had housed thousands of soldiers en route to war became – initially with few improvements – the Bonegilla Migrant Centre, home to 309,000 migrants between 1947 and 1971. Largest and longest-lasting of Australia's migrant reception centres, it was opened as the Bonegilla

Migrant Experience Heritage Park in 2010. It's estimated that more than 1.5 million Australians are descended from those who passed through. Many were former enemies.

One POW who did return to Germany was Jacob Rosel, captured in Eritrea in January 1941. He arrived in Australia in the *Queen Elizabeth* in August 1941 and was interned at Murchison, central Victoria until returning to Germany in 1947. Who knows, he might have been a distant relative.

He was a lucky German soldier – not so fortunate was **Field Marshal Erwin Rommel**, respected by his enemies ('The Desert Fox'), less so by his megalomaniac Fuhrer. When Rommel's links to the conspirators of the Generals' Plot which came close to assassinating Hitler in 1944 became known, Rommel was given the choice of committing suicide (being assured that his family would not be persecuted) or facing a trial that would bring disgrace and execution. He took cyanide. (His son Manfred was to write a foreword for Peter Fitzsimons' history, *Tobruk*.)

The Manresa tennis courts – a perfect site for the first generation of ugly flats – vanished in the early 60s.

John Rosel's albums were occasionally brought into the light by kids trying to read between the lines. **His camera** vanished in the early 60s once the author obtained one of those newfangled Japanese cameras.

Lord Haw-Haw was a generic term of mockery applied to Germany's propaganda broadcasters, especially the US-born Briton, William Joyce. He was hanged for treason at Wandsworth Prison, London, in January 1946.

Students from Wangaratta High School drove 250 km to join Alan Macfarlane OAM EM (centre), President of the 2/24th Battalion Association, at the Anzac Day march in Melbourne in 2009. The battalion has been known as 'Wangaratta's Own' since it commenced training there in 1940. Photograph courtesy of Faye Macfarlane.

Tobruk, 2009: Harry Frazer's daughter, Christina Westmore-Peyton, at the Fig Tree, where caves sheltered a regimental aid post. The tree, the only foliage on the featureless desert inside the Tobruk defences, was a navigation point for troops. It survived the shells and bombs of both sides as fighting ebbed and flowed.

* * *

This journey with the men of the 2/24th makes it possible to appreciate a little of what they endured, if not the postwar impacts on their mental wellbeing.

Americans characterise those who endured the Depression and WWII as 'The Great Generation'. Better, perhaps, The Stoic Generation, with duty done in war and peace, unflinchingly and usually without complaint.

John Rosel, to us a towering figure, kept the faith – literally and metaphorically – despite losing his Lorna and Peter.

Yet we can still only guess at the range of emotions he experienced in those wild three days at Tobruk.

He died bravely without ever opening up about combat, surely a central experience of his life. In that respect only, the refrain from an antiwar version of a popular American Civil War marching song keeps nagging: 'Johnny, I hardly knew ya.'

ACKNOWLEDGMENTS AND THANKS

Mark Johnston, historian and patient guide to arcane Army issues, author of 11 WWII Australian Army histories: https://www.markjohnstonhistorian.com/books.html.

Christina Westmore-Peyton: by making available her father's letters from Tobruk, Christina gives Australians a human insight into the siege. We thank her for lodging the letters with the Australian War Memorial (PRO 1943), and her generosity in letting me draw on his letters and photographs, and her memories of her father. christinawestmore@bigpond.com.

Alastair Davison, honorary secretary, 2/24 Battalion Association (secretary@2-24 battalion.org.au).

Australian War Memorial: historian Karl James, and Jennie Norberry at the Reading Room.

Australian National Archives, Melbourne: Gerard Poed.

John Tidey, Jeremy Bourke, Bill Clancy, Noel Carrick, Bruce King, Adrienne Jones, for encouragement, deft editing and friendship.

David Rosel, for Natimuk research and photography.

BIBLIOGRAPHY AND SOURCES

Published sources

Cochrane, Peter, *Tobruk 1941,* ABC Books, 2002.

Fitzsimons, Peter, *Tobruk*, Harper Collins, 2006, 2009.

Maughan, Barton, *Tobruk and El Alamein*, Australian War Memorial, 1966.

Moorehead, Alan, *The Desert War*, Hamish Hamilton, 1965.

Rosel, Mike and Gerry, *The Old Golden Days*, Focus Print Group, 2017 (family history).

Serle, R.P., *2/24: A History of the 2/24 Australian Infantry Battalion*, Jacaranda Press, 1963.

Wilmot, Chester, *Tobruk*, Angus and Robertson, 1944.

Websites

Australian War Memorial.

Australian National Archives.

Unpublished sources

Lt John Rosel, two albums of WWII photographs, and service records.

Interview with Tobruk veteran, Lt Alan Macfarlane, May 2013 (former President of the 2/24th Battalion Association).

Interview with Ray Walker ('Uncle Ray'), Tobruk colleague and fellow Demons tragic at the MCG.

Recollections of family and friends.

INDEX

www.ingramcontent.com/pod-product-compliance
Ingram Content Group Australia Pty Ltd
76 Discovery Rd, Dandenong South VIC 3175, AU
AUHW020135130726
429791AU00003B/123

9 781925 984743